EST MARATHON '98
The One-Act Plays

SMITH AND KRAUS PUBLISHERS
Contemporary Playwrights / Collections

Act One Festival '94
Act One Festival '95

EST Marathon '94: The One-Act Plays
EST Marathon '95: The One-Act Plays
EST Marathon '96: The One-Act Plays
EST Marathon '97: The One-Act Plays

Humana Festival: 20 One-Acts Plays 1976–1996
Humana Festival '93: The Complete Plays
Humana Festival '94: The Complete Plays
Humana Festival '95: The Complete Plays
Humana Festival '96: The Complete Plays
Humana Festival '97: The Complete Plays
Humana Festival '98: The Complete Plays

Women Playwrights: The Best Plays of 1992
Women Playwrights: The Best Plays of 1993
Women Playwrights: The Best Plays of 1994
Women Playwrights: The Best Plays of 1995
Women Playwrights: The Best Plays of 1996
Women Playwrights: The Best Plays of 1997
Women Playwrights: The Best Plays of 1998

If you require pre-publication information about upcoming Smith and Kraus books, you may receive our semi-annual catalogue, free of charge, by sending your name and address to *Smith and Kraus Catalogue, 4 Lower Mill Road, North Stratford, NH 03590. Or call us at (800) 895-4331, fax (603) 922-3348. WWW.SmithKraus.com.*

EST MARATHON '98
The One-Act Plays

CONTEMPORARY PLAYWRIGHTS
SERIES

SK
A Smith and Kraus Book

A Smith and Kraus Book
Published by Smith and Kraus, Inc.
PO Box 127, Lyme, NH 03768

Copyright ©1999 by Smith and Kraus
All rights reserved
Manufactured in the United States of America
Cover and Text Design by Julia Hill Gignoux

First Edition: August 1999
10 9 8 7 6 5 4 3 2 1

The Library of Congress Cataloging-In-Publication Data

EST Marathon '98: the one-act plays / edited by Marisa Smith. —1st ed.
    p.   cm.   — (Contemporary playwrights series) ISSN 1067-9510
    ISBN 1-57525-165-5

    1. One-act plays, American. 2. American drama—20th century. 3. Ensemble Studio Theater.
    I. Smith, Marisa. II. Series.

PS627.053E88   1995
812'.04108—dc20
                                95-2287
                                 CIP

CONTENTS

Dream

BY BILLY ARONSON

THE AUTHOR

Billy Aronson's plays have been honored with publication in *Best American Short Plays 92–93* and a New York Foundation for the Arts grant, and are performed frequently at Ensemble Studio Theater. His new play, *The Art Room,* is being produced at the Woolly Mammoth Theatre, and published in the upcoming volume *Plays From The Woolly Mammoth.* His writing for the musical theater includes the original concept and additional lyrics for *Rent,* and the librettos for a pair of operas commissioned by American Opera Projects, with music by Rusty Magee and Kitty Brazelton. TV writing credits include various shows for MTV, Comedy Central, Nickelodeon, PBS, A&E, and Children's Television Workshop.

ORIGINAL PRODUCTION

Dream was first produced at the Ensemble Studio Theatre, in Marathon '98, the 21st Annual Festival of One-Act Plays (Curt Dempster, Artistic Director; Jamie Richards, Executive Producer) in New York City, June, 1998. The production was directed by Jamie Richards, assistant directed by Delora Whitney, and stage managed by Erica Briggs, with costumes designed by Amela Baksic, set by Austin K. Sanderson, lighting by Greg MacPherson, sound by Laura Grace Brown, props by Stephanie Summerville, with the following cast:

WOMAN. . . . . Joanna P. Adler
MONSTER . . . . Peter Lewis

AUTHOR'S NOTE

I'd like to thank the fearless cast, crew, producers, and designers who worked on the premiere of "Dream"; the many gifted actors who auditioned, each of whom taught me something about the play; Peter Wallace, Ellen Mareneck, and Brad Bellamy who helped develop the play in Octoberfest; my agent Beth Blickers; my wife Lisa Vogel; and my entire EST family, for working on my scripts with such passion and commitment, and always asking for the next one.

—Billy Aronson

CHARACTERS

WOMAN
MONSTER

Woman spoons ice cream from a carton. Behind her, observing: Monster. Sound effect: ringing alarm.

WOMAN: So you're what. A cross between King Kong, my old boss, and Godzilla?

Don't know, and I don't care, 'cause that was the snooze alarm. Any moment beeping, music, second alarm, then I'm up and running, and you're a former whatever.

No, this will not be a nightmare. My last pre-morning dream will remain pleasant throughout, thanks to my endless supply of sweet and luscious, non-fattening, non-filling, non-everything ice cream.

You can't compete, so pop.

Still here?

(Monster moves downward into a crouch.)

WOMAN: Down, dropping down. Rain today, that's right, ninety percent. Drip drop, car's in the shop, so I can't drop off the kids.

So what. Kids're fine on foot. Gavin's got a poncho. Gretta's got a poncho. Gavin's got boots. Gretta's got—fuck. Gretta's boot is gaping, since she stepped on the tack. Her foot was fine so I ignored the hole, it tore and grew til the whole boot flaps like a jowl. So the walk, she'll soak, sock sopping, squelching the skin, little toes gripping and squishing and slopping through shoes down halls to class to sit, shiver, shiver, shit.

Rummage for her old pair, force in the foot? She'll scream bloody murder.

Rummage for Gavin's old pair? Stuff with socks, let her wobble?

Wait.

Neighbor's spare pair. Lynn's kids are with Chris. Little Jenny's Gretta's exact same size.

But. But.

Can't beg Lynn for boots after denying her butter. She understood, but still.

Plus I owe her a plunger. You can't boot-beg a neighbor after denying her butter and misplacing a plunger.

Hold everything. That plunger sucked. Lynn's lucky we lost it. Who'd bring up a two-buck sucky plunger?

So: upon waking: sprint to Lynn's. Apologize for the hour. Make light of the butter. Beg for the boots. If she brings up the plunger, guffaw.

(Woman guffaws, returns to ice cream.)

Let nothing come between us.

(Monster somersaults.)

WOMAN: I'm on a roll at work, so what.

Getting my name around. Survived the summer assault, so they bounced me up to thirty-seven.

So why the negative spin? There's no summer assault this fall. Anything but tumbling, I'm soaring towards the gold. What screwy stunt could possibly—fuck. The new code. At nine the new code hits the floor.

I'll be boggled. Sure, the others'll whine about being hindered. Fuck them. If they're hindered they can catch up over lunch or stay late. But I have to car-fetch after lunch and Gavin-grab later, so catch-up or stay late I absolutely can't.

I'll be stuck sweating. Eyeballs watching fingers clutching fingers. I'll lose my zip and flounder. When my peers get the nod I'll be left back. They'll be bounced to forty-four, I'll sink to twenty-five, twenty-three, twelve, where I'll snivel through the minutia of a million rancid afternoons crammed with forced conversations, smile-faking, face aching, cheeks sagging, flesh dripping to the floor til I slump, forever frozen by a code with no hope of escape—unless after boot-getting I skip shower, scarf toast, kiss kids, cut to bus, car-fetch first, drive to work, slip into systems, trade pastry for code-clues, code-conquer through lunch, then cruise on ahead, secure on the floor.

(Woman returns to ice cream.)

I'm back.

(Monster rises to his feet, moves in a curving path.)

WOMAN: Figure eight?

The thing for Kate. Our women thing. Stephanie said she'll host, if I'll invite the eight.

But if I haven't figured the eight by tonight, no thing.

No problem. The eight'll be easy.

Kate. Me. Stephanie.

Kate. Me. Stephanie. Beth. Sharon. Sue. Lynn. Harriet.

Yes.

Wait.

Beth hates Harriet. Stephanie can take or leave Harriet. Got to cut Harriet.

Can't cut Har. Har's out-there. Kate needs out-there. Without Har, we'll have no out-there thing.

Jan's out-there. Nobody hates Jan.

Kate. Me. Stephanie. Beth. Sharon. Sue. Lynn. Jan.

Yes.

Wait.

Jan sees Ben. Sharon sees Ben. Stephanie saw Ben. Cut Jan. Call out-there Jennifer.

Kate Me Steph Beth Shar Sue Lynn Jen.

Yes.

Shit.

Jen talks to Cyn. Cyn talks to Har. Har'd be miffed if she knew she was cut.

Cut Jen? Can't. No out-there without her.

Keep Har, cut Beth?

Kate Me Steph Shar Sue Lynn Jen Har?

Can't cut Beth. Beth and Steph go back.

Can't cut Shar. Shar sees Sue. Sue sees Lynn. Lynn is in. Sue's in. Shar's in. Jen's in. Har's in. Beth's miffed. Kate's crushed. I'm screwed. Shit. Unless…

Cut Sue.

Since Sue moved Lynn can't keep up with Sue. So if Lynn and Cyn stay Har-free, Sue won't know she's cut and be crushed.

Kate Me Steph Beth Shar Lynn Cyn Jen.

Eureka.

I'll run the eight by Steph at nine, get to Kate before noon when she heads out of town, but if Steph's running late she'll call back after one, so Kate's noon is too soon and Steph's nine is too late and so so so so so: Skip toast. No choice.

Get boot, skip shower, check Steph, skip toast, kiss kids, skip bus, cab to car-fetch, sprint to systems, pastry for code-clues, code-conquer, call Kate.

(Woman returns to ice cream.)

That was close.

(Monster starts to take off his head.)

(Woman shrieks.)

(Monster starts to take off his head.)

WOMAN: Absolutely no, Guy's not about to head off.

(Monster starts to take off his head.)

WOMAN: So what are you saying that Tuesday at the diner when I said "summer" he looked at his pork chop a second too soon like on the park-walk when I pointed out orchids and he let go his grip? Well he didn't, it wasn't, and he's not about to take off.

So I will definitely not spend a summer dumped. I will definitely not, while watching some idiotic talk show, have to explain to the kids why I'm sobbing. I will definitely not find myself dodging my reflection, or jerking back from the table, or vomiting my feelings all over the Meadowlands.

(Monster starts to take off his head.)

WOMAN: All right so if he is drifting just a bit maybe maybe I could maybe if I thanked him for the paperback—

I should have really thanked him sure but I was thinking shit when am I gonna have the time to read a stupid—

shit.

He prob'ly loved the movie so his giving me the paperback was a gesture of genuine—

Well it's never too late to slip in a belated thanks over coffee, and then he'll glance up, and I'll be looking, he'll pause, and I'll gush til he's totally through drifting off.

(Monster starts to take off his head.)

WOMAN: No no when he glances I shouldn't be looking, increase the tension, supply and demand, so my eyes'll be busy with coffee, to set up a super-charged gush.

(Monster starts to take off his head.)

WOMAN: Or if eyes aren't the key then it must be it must be the shoulders, can't slouch like a dog but always and always pull back so my angles say upward and bold towards the sky free and fresh, or no no have my brows clipped, ears tucked, lips reversed, guts removed—

(Monster starts to take off his head.)

WOMAN: Can you really be still heading off?—or is this about work I'll be yanked, left to crawl back to postal where they'll cough up my com-ments or grovel to intake where they'll stomp on my record, it's too late to change areas, how'll we eat?—or no no you're ripping open 'cause I'll be exposed to my friends, my inner workings, all the corners I've cut in conversation, blown secrets, bent facts, secret pacts all revealed til I'm a despicable liar left sweating alone—Or the kids tuh tuh tuh torn away?, because of the four seconds a day when they're not cuh cuh cuh covered?, the tuh tuh traffic-jam scheduling-fuckup? the juh juh juh genetic-flaw leaves them puh puh puh poisoned and suh suh suh screaming and kih kih kih kih—

Look, this isn't constructive. I can compensate for a boot or slap a scab over a new code. But I can't occupy three lives at the same moment, assume a new set of natural abilities, or make a man want to return to the same bed til he dies, I'm not a sorcerer or a dictator, so be tactful.

(Monster starts to take off his head.)

(Woman shrieks. Woman returns to ice cream, shrieks. Woman turns over carton, pours out: monster fur. Woman roars, charges Monster, pommels him, finally sinks, exhausted.)

WOMAN: You're more concrete than I am.

(Woman grovels to Monster.)

Yes I'm completely powerless to stomp you out because I'm a limbless slab of nothing. Happy?

(Sound effect: Beeping. Booming voice, garbled and distant, emits a few syllables.)

WOMAN: The radio, at last. So I'm almost free from—

(Monster takes off his head, his costume falls away revealing: a man.)

MONSTER: Rubbatussin.

WOMAN: Donny Green?

(Sound effect: A few chords of sweet music, vague and distant.)

WOMAN: Donny Green. We're not twelve any more, huh. Where'd you disappear to? I wrote your new school but every letter came back. Thought I'd bump into you on the avenue, at the drug store or the field, but I never saw you anywhere, though I could feel you watching me everywhere, from the mirror, the clock, the sparkling particles on my window on winter nights, that was you, watching over me, and even here you've been watching, from behind my worst nightmare, just like at the school fair, that grisly moment, when Robyn and Karen had deserted me, and the twins were out sick, so I was stuck walking by myself, alone past the relay races, the sponge toss, the cotton candy stand, til you appeared with a cup of punch that we said tasted like something but we couldn't figure what, then your friends dragged you away, but you reappeared and said Rubbatussin, and I said Rubbatussin right Rubbatussin, and you took my elbow and kissed my eyelashes and the sky swooped down it was night in a painting, and the candy apples, and the crushed lemons, and the kids doing the crab walk swirled 'round as we stepped through it all, as if nothing could touch me, not Robyn and Karen, not the girls in seven K who said I was phoney, not Mister Gone's mocking my vowels, fifth period tennis, last seat in band, all the scabs in my hair, all the whispering in the world couldn't slay me because your hand holding mine said everything would be fine forever, and everything will be fine forever.

MONSTER: Rubbatussin.

WOMAN: Guy would never head out, and if he does I'll find somebody, and if work slows down the kids'll get by, colds pass, it might not even rain, the morning might be glorious since you're back in my arms again, making make me feel brand new, the only light this empty room has ever had, I want to hold you til I die I long to be close to you.

(Sound effect: Beeping.)

WOMAN: I need you more today than yesterday.

(Sound effect: More beeping.)

WOMAN: There never seems to be the time to say the things we want to say once we find them.

(Sound effect: Long beep. Silence.)

WOMAN: Next comes the last alarm. In an instant you'll vanish, and I'll jerk awake, cursing myself for taking you seriously.

MONSTER: Rubbatussin.

(He takes her elbow, kisses her eyelashes. They hold hands and sway.)

WOMAN: This magic moment will last forever.

END OF PLAY

Mary MacGregor

BY KEITH ALAN BENJAMIN

FOR ANNE O'SULLIVAN
MY TRUE LOVE. ALWAYS, AND FOREVER.

THE AUTHOR

Mr. Benjamin's most recent play, *Mary MacGregor,* was produced for Marathon '98, The Ensemble Studio Theatre's renowned festival of one-act plays. Three of his one-acts have appeared in EST's Octoberfest ('95, '96, '97). A fourth was presented at Naked Angels in their "Tuesdays at 9:00" series. Mr. Benjamin is a graduate of the Berklee College of Music in Boston and the Neighborhood Playhouse School of Theatre in NYC. He also studied privately with Sanford Meisner. Mr. Benjamin is a member of the Dramatist's Guild, Inc.

ORIGINAL PRODUCTION

Mary MacGregor was first produced at the Ensemble Studio Theatre, in Marathon '98, the 21st Annual Festival of One-Act Plays (Curt Dempster, Artistic Director; Jamie Richards, Executive Producer) in New York City in June, 1998. It was directed by Joe White. Lighting design by Greg MacPherson, scenic design by Ann Waugh, costume by Julie Doyle, and the stage manager was Marina Bridges. The cast was as follows:

DAVID . . . . Andrew Weems
MARY . . . . Anne O'Sullivan

AUTHOR'S NOTE

Mary's dialogue is a continuous monologue and no attempt should be made to arbitrarily find pauses for David to speak. Much of this dialogue is to be spoken simultaneously. It is the director and actors' duty to find the natural pauses and rhythms (based, in part, on the activities that Mary does throughout the play). That will allow the fluidity of the play. I encourage all such persons to experiment with the interplay and overlapping dialogue of these characters.

No particular ethnicity is required for these parts. Any actors, in almost any age range, are eligible to perform these characters.

AUDIO NOTE

When Mary turns on the Boom Box, the music should *not* continue to play until she shuts it off. The music should begin a slow fade when she says "I love this piece," and should be off by the time she says "…To you…about us, about…" It should fade back up starting at "It was a secret bond between me and Claire." This keeps the music from becoming a distraction during this section of the play.

CHARACTERS
MARY
DAVID

PLACE
An apartment on the Upper West Side in Manhattan.

TIME
The Present

As the lights come up we see David seated on a sofa center stage working on a crossword puzzle. The room is almost empty except for some packing boxes and a boom box. Mary is seen crossing back and forth through the open doorway to the bedroom and she begins talking from there.

MARY: Jesus, how many T-shirts can one man have? I mean didn't we get rid of a couple of boxes of these things just a few months ago? Do they copulate while they sit in those drawers? Well, the thrift store will certainly appreciate them. *(She crosses the doorway carrying a pile of T-shirts.)* The next time I see some homeless person with an SS Titanic Crew Member T-shirt on, we can both feel good. I'm going to keep this one, though, it's ugly, but that trip to Idyllwild was so beautiful that's all I think of when I see it. You'd want me to keep this one, I know. *(She crosses the doorway again with a T-shirt.)* Oh, I met the new tenant on Monday, she's this nice young girl from California who wants to be in the theatre, so she's broke, of course. Have you ever noticed that a lot of people in the theatre seems to come from really privileged or really impoverished backgrounds? The decline of the middle class, that's the proof of it. Anyway, I'm leaving her the sofa and the coffee table. She was thrilled, she's got no furniture at all. Oh, and the bed, I'm leaving her the bed. I knew you wouldn't mind. They were never your favorites. You always liked that modern stuff, leather and chrome. *(She crosses the doorway again.)* God, you fought tooth and nail with me to bring that junk over here. Good thing real taste won out. But I really don't need this stuff now and neither do you, so it's nice to be able to help someone else out as they start over.

(Mary has come out of the bedroom, David ignores her and continues working on the puzzle. Mary dumps some T-shirts next to the boxes and returns to the bedroom while still talking. She comes back out carrying a small urn containing David's ashes. She places it on a small table near the sofa and goes to fold and pack T-shirts.)

MARY: I saw Ron and Annie yesterday and gave them my new address. It was nice to bump into them again under normal circumstances. I hadn't seen them since the funeral.

(For the first time, David looks up.)

MARY: They're leaving the city you know. Annie's pregnant and Ronnie just got promoted, so they're getting some place up on the Hudson, near Cold Spring. I said I'd be sure to visit them once they got settled in. I just can't imagine Ronnie commuting every day, but he's put on a lot of

weight this year, and with what hair he's still got going gray, he is begin-
ning to look more and more like the perfect commuter. *(She walks to
downstage window.)*

DAVID: Ronnie's been a commuter for a long time. He's got some young thing
up in Yonkers he's been doing twice a week for the last two years. She's
Italian, she feeds him pasta everytime. No wonder he's put on weight.
She's not only squeezed those love handles, she created them.

MARY: The leaves are really changing fast now in the park. *(She walks back to
the sofa and sits.)* You know how it is here, four months of oppressive
summer, four months of oppressive winter, three and a half months of
obscure gray that's neither here nor there, and two really beautiful days
of fall, when the leaves are as colorful as anything you have to drive miles
to see. I was thinking…maybe you and I could go up there tonight for
our last walk. I mean, I know that's what you wanted. You always told
me "When I die, just spread my ashes in Central Park." I could never
figure out why that meant so much to you.

DAVID: Hey, rent free on the upper west side for eternity, are you kidding?

MARY: *(She eyes a half empty bottle of scotch near the sofa and pours herself a
drink.)* Well, I'm not going to bother to pack this. How about a drink
before we go? What should we drink to?

DAVID: How about to me? Cause guess what, I've stopped smoking!

MARY: *(She clinks the glass to the urn and drinks.)* Here's to us baby, you and
me, and to all the dreams we had together.

DAVID: That was a joke. I've stopped smoking. Don't you get it? Cremation?
Smoking? Forget it. Even when I was alive you never heard me, you
never got my jokes.

MARY: Oh, Jesus, David, why didn't you take better care of yourself? You
knew heart disease ran in your family, why couldn't you have jogged in
the park, rather than just sit there, why couldn't you have changed your
diet just a little bit? *(She takes a sip of her drink.)*

DAVID: You're right, I should have stuck with the turkey bacon.

MARY: Why couldn't you have eased off the drinking just a bit?

DAVID: Here we go. Health lectures as she hoists another round of scotch.
The MacGregor double standard lives on.

MARY: *(She pours herself some more scotch and returns to the boxes.)* I mean, one
moment you're there at the office with Ronnie and Claire fighting about
the next project, and then you're just gone.

DAVID: Yes well, let's not forget the exciting, and I might add, expensive EMS
taxi to the hospital, but let's not split hairs now.

MARY:

(As she rearranges and packs boxes.)

And goddamnit, the last thing we ever talked about was that stupid Visa bill. That was it, our last conversation, and what was it about? Who made the decision to get four side tables instead of two. And I started yelling at you, and you got quiet in that snarky kind of way you do when you know you're wrong but can't admit it, and then you went off to bed and that was it. I stormed around the living room for half an hour, and when I came into bed you were already asleep. We didn't touch each other all night, and the next morning you got up early and went to work and I never saw you again. I don't want to get morbid here, Jesus, I'm sorry, I don't want to be this way, here, I'll just have another drink, and put on some music.*(She fills up her glass and goes downstage to the boom box.)* I left some tapes out. Packing music, you know. I never really listened to music until I met you. I mean, I loved to go bars and dance, but I never just sat down and listened to music until I met you. I remember you saying "you don't hear music with your ears, you hear it with your

DAVID:

"Snarky?" Where'd you come up with "snarky?"
I wasn't wrong, I…
(David rises and moves upstage to the table.)

Your favorite trick to get my attention.

Good idea.

(David moves downstage, standing over Mary as she sifts through her tapes.)
Oh great, any Miles Davis in there? I sure hope I get to meet him soon.

True enough.

heart," and although I knew what you were saying it took a long time for me to experience it that way, but you took me there. *(Mary turns the tape player on. David smiles and moves behind the sofa, listening.)* That's how I really traveled with you. *(She sits on the arm of the sofa.)* There was something you showed me about yourself that only surfaced when we heard music together and I'd laugh at you, I know it was terrible, but the sight of you crying while playing Kind of Blue was just too much for me. I guess it was hard for me to see just how deeply you felt some things. It scared me, I don't know why, I guess all that stuff about women wanting sensitive men is a little different when you're sitting in a room watching a grown man weep to Kind of Blue. *(She drinks some more.)* I love this piece. I always wanted to dance with you, but you never would. You said you couldn't dance, and I guess that was true. *(She touches the urn.)* Funny, you had such grace when you made love, but in public you always seemed awkward. *(She takes her drink and heads back to packing.)* I always said to Claire that there was a secret side of you that nobody saw but

You were a good traveler Mary, you always were.

(He's embarrassed by this.)
Oh God, not this again.

Maybe you were afraid of two Marys living in the same house.

Well, I couldn't.

True, true.
Oh, thanks.

me. Claire always saw that though. She got you more than anybody except me. She always said you were sexy, that she could feel what you must be like in bed. I like that she felt that. I guess that's why we're so close, Claire and me. I mean, she knew things about my life without even having me explain them. Like the night you called from Los Angeles on business to tell me that you'd be there another three weeks. I was devastated. I felt like I was never going to see you again, and she held me in her arms and I sobbed, I just collapsed in her arms, and she didn't say anything to me at first. She just held me. She's the only other person I know who understands silence the way you do. I hate silence, well obviously, listen to me carry on this way, but you and Claire really feel at ease with silence. It's still hard for me, but now and then I get it. I don't run away from it. I don't try to fill it with TV's and telephones, I just try and let it take me wherever it's going. It's really hard right now, I just think of all the things we could have said to each other in those spaces. I mean, now I can add up exactly how many

Yeah, well that's true about any couple, Mary, not just us. *(He moves about the room, uncomfortably.)*

Mary, can we not talk about Claire right now? Jesus.

She knew about your life alright.

I'm sorry.

You're always so dramatic.

No!

Not right now, I don't.

I never told you about Claire and me did I?

days, hours, and minutes we had together, exactly, and I start thinking about what I'd give to fill some of those silences with words. To you. About us. About...Claire says you and I...I never told you about Claire and me, did I? Sometimes I wanted to, I thought about telling you, I kept picturing the proper time and place, but it never happened. I love Claire, I think I always will, but there was that time, maybe two years ago, you know, when you were out in L.A., when I was so lonely, so bereft for you, like now, and Claire was there for me, holding me, kissing me, on my eyes, my lips. It just happened. I needed to be touched. I needed somebody's warmth. I'd never been with a woman before. Claire had. She told me later. Maybe that's why it felt so safe with her. She knew how scared I was. She knew how to calm me. She stayed all night, with me, in our bed. I didn't know what to say in the morning. I didn't know what to do. I didn't feel guilty, I just felt, different. Claire was so sweet. She lay back in the bed while I fumbled for something to say, naked on top of the sheets, smiling at me and as I kept sputtering she

I'll talk louder OK? Maybe then you can hear me. *(He moves behind Mary and sits in the chair.)* Didn't I just say that? Can you hear me now? And what the fuck do you mean "Claire and I"? Alright, I'll just say it—I slept with Claire— once, OK? I loved Claire, I thought. I guess in some ways I still do.
That's when I knew it was wrong. I was so lonely. I felt like I wasn't sexual anymore, and there was Claire, and...

...it just happened.

I'd never been with another woman.

leaned over and kissed me deeply, slowly and climbed out of the bed and went into the bathroom. That was it. We made breakfast, and drank mimosas, and then she left. And I was happy. When you finally got back from L.A., I felt guilty at first, like I betrayed you. But as the weeks passed I felt really good about it. It was a secret bond between me and Claire. She never asked me to hide it from you, that was me, but whenever we fought or I felt us drifting apart, I'd think about that night. Oh Jesus, this music reminds me of you. *(She goes to the boom-box and turns up the volume.)* Remember how I'd dance for you? Remember how you'd make us those special rum drinks of yours, and you'd put on some music, and I just had to dance for you? I want to dance for you, right now, right now, my baby. It's almost like you're here. *(Mary pretends David is lying on the sofa, and dances facing him, she dances around the room, returns to the sofa and accidentally knocks the urn to the floor.)* Oh my God oh my God Goddammit Goddammit David my David you can't leave me. *(She cradles the urn in her arms.)* I want to feel you. I want to see you, I want

I was miserable.

I felt guilty, like I betrayed you.

You did?
Yeah, I'll say.

Jesus, you and Claire. I always thought something like that might turn me on, but Jesus, Claire?

Don't try to cheer me up now, please.

Yeah, I remember.
(David leaps onto the sofa facing Mary.)
How about, better than almost? What can I do to get through to you? *(David stands on the sofa and dances with Mary.)* Yep, you really can dance—and I really can't.
It's ok, it's ok, I'm fine, really—see?
(He leans over her.)
I don't want to leave you.
Mary, look at me, I'm right

to touch you. Oh God. I can't
do this. Oh, David please hold
me, please just hold me.
(She collapses to the floor.)
I'm all alone. Oh God, I'm all
alone. Oh David please
touch me please touch me
I have to feel you.
*(She opens the urn and
places her fingers inside.)*
I want to be you David, I want
to be you.
*(She slowly brushes her
forehead, her cheeks, and her
neck with the ashes.)*
Don't leave me here David,
please don't leave me. If we
go to the park, can't I spread
my ashes too? Can't I come
with you? I want to come with
you. Let's both disappear into
the world…oh, David I'm
sorry. I'm sorry about so many
things. I know I was pushy,
well, sometimes, I mean, you
needed to be pushed, and
could be a pain in the ass. I
know, I know, but oh, how I
loved you. I know what it's
like to really love someone
now, thanks to you. You taught
me. Teach me now how to let go.
I have to let go, I have to let
you go. But I have to keep you
with me always, always. I
don't know what it is. I don't
know what I'm feeling right
now, but it has something to do
with making you a part of my

here.
Mary, I can't, goddamn it, I
can't. Mary, I'm ok.
Please don't cry.
No you're not, you're not. Mary I'm
here, I'm right here beside
you. Can't you feel me?
*(He tries to cradle her in
his arms, she slips through.)*
Can't you feel me?
Shit! Fuck! God Damn It!

Mary, fuck the ashes, they
aren't me. I'm here.

Yes, let's do it. Let's go
together. Just tell me what to
do. Jesus, tell me what to do.
I'm all alone now too. Just
tell me what to do.
Me too.
Sometimes?

Yeah, well…

I can't.

Always, and forever.

With…

life, everyday, about rejoicing
in the time we had together.
It's something about trying to
use what I learned with you in
my life, not lighting some
fucking candle every year on
the day you died but maybe,
maybe, lighting a candle
everyday from now on so that I
keep your spirit with me, no,
in me everyday of my life. I
don't know what I'm saying, I
don't...I don't...oh God
David, I wish I could feel you
here with me right now, so I
can get off this fucking floor
and take you to the park.
Where does it come from? Where
does the strength to live what
I'm saying come from? Are you
going to fade from me, like
everything else does with time?
Am I going to think less and
less about you as the years go
by? The years. I've never
been so frightened of living as
I am at this moment. Years
without you. Will you remember
me? Can you remember me? Do
you see me sitting here? What
are you feeling my love, what
are you feeling right now? I
wish I was sure where we went
when we die. I wished I
believed some religion, *any*
religion. I'd say a million
fucking Hail Mary's just to
feel I knew what was happening
to you right now. It's funny,

It is?

Really?

I am.

OK, OK, whatever you want.

I don't know.

No, I don't think so...

Absolutely not, not you.

Oh God, Mary, of course.
Yes, yes. Yes.

I'm feeling really, really sad.

Me too.

(He stands and moves upstage.)
I don't know, but, it's funny,

you feel so close to me, yet so far away. Will you walk with me, my baby, my love? Will you put your arms around me as we walk through the park one last time? I'll come back there, I will, but I know you won't be there. You'll be here. You'll be everywhere, and nowhere, but somehow, that's going to be alright. *(She gets herself up from the floor.)* It's going to be OK because…me living is you living, and as long as I'm here, you are too, and, aw fuck it David, let's just go, OK? *(She picks up her jacket, bag and finally the urn.)* *(With quiet acceptance.)* I'm ready, I really am. *(She exits. David follows behind her.)*

I feel kind of like, like, I have to go soon. Isn't that weird?

Sure Mary. Let's go to the park, one last time.

Yeah, well…

Because, me living is like you living.
I'm here.
Ok baby. You're going to be alright Mary MacGregor. Trust me.

END OF PLAY

How to Plant a Rose

BY ELIZABETH DIGGS

THE AUTHOR
Elizabeth Diggs is the author of *Nightingale, Close Ties, Goodbye Freddy, American Beef, Dumping Ground* and other plays, produced in New York at the Vineyard Theatre and EST, and at many theatres in the U.S. and in Europe. She also wrote the book for a musical, *Mirette* (with Tom Jones and Harvey Schmidt). Awards include playwriting fellowships from the Guggenheim Foundation and the N.E.A., a Los Angeles DramaLogue award for playwrighting, the CBS / FDG prize and a Kennedy Center—Fund for New American Plays grant.

ORIGINAL PRODUCTION
How to Plant a Rose was first produced at the Ensemble Studio Theatre, in Marathon '98, the 21st Annual Festival of One-Act Plays (Curt Dempster, Artistic Director; Jamie Richards, Executive Producer) in New York City in June, 1998. It was directed by Mark Roberts. The cast was as follows:

GARDENER . . . . Delphi Harrington

CHARACTERS
GARDENER: seventies

Gardener enters. A wheelbarrow is half filled with soil; as well as a pick-ax, shovel, pruners, several paper bags and a watering can. She's in her garden. She speaks to the audience—and to herself.

GARDENER: All right, we're going to plant a rose—
(Holds it up, displaying bare roots and three stubby canes about six inches long.)

Doesn't look like much. But in just a few weeks it will send out long, supple luminous new shoots, sometimes six inches in a day! That's one of the great things about roses—surprise.

People are wary of roses. They think they're delicate, require endless attention. This is true, but the opposite is true too. Roses are hardy— they will survive draught, flood, and pestilence. Almost anything you can say about a rose is true, because roses are like life.

A lot of people remember a rose from their childhood, maybe the scent of sweetness and sunshine, or just a glimpse of an old rambling rose sprawled over a fence. Maybe a memory is what will inspire you to plant your first rose.

My Grandfather Quincy had a rose garden. He planted his first rose in 1907 in Tulsa. People told him roses wouldn't grow out there—the weather is too fierce. The wind blows off the plains in the Spring at sixty miles an hour, filled with dust. But he remembered a red rose that bloomed every Spring after frigid New England winters in his aunt's garden. So he took a cutting and planted it near the back porch behind his first little house in Tulsa.

My grandfather—Charles Quincy—was a hopeful man. He was poor but educated—a Ph.D. chemist. When he heard about the discovery of a huge oil field out in Indian Territory, he decided to go and offer his services.

So he left New England and went out West with his new wife. She was from Richmond, Virginia—Rose Elizabeth Kenworthy—an old Virginia family, left penniless after the Civil War. Her beauty and her name were all the fortune she had, and that was enough for him. Soon they had a son, Robert Kenworthy, named in honor of Rose Elizabeth's heritage—Kenworthy for her father who was killed at Shiloh, and Robert for the general who lost the war.

Fall is the best time to plant a rose, when the plant is dormant. You want to give it a good place to sleep through the winter and store up strength for Spring.

First you dig a big hole, two feet deep and two feet across. For this you need a pick and a shovel to get through the clay and rocks. This is a hard workout, but satisfying.

Planting a rose is a solitary act. You want to be free and alone to contend with the earth.

By the year 1912, Charles Quincy was making a good living advising wildcatters about the chemical properties of oil. He and Rose Elizabeth built a big two-story white frame house. He dug up the red rose—it took him several hours—and transplanted it. That year, their second child was born—Virginia. That was my mother.

In a few years, the red rose from Massachusetts was ten feet tall, and every Spring it must have blossomed with three hundred roses. People came to see it. Charles had gotten pretty confident about roses. (He learned that his aunt's rose was a hybrid perpetual called American Beauty, bred in 1875.) He wanted to put in a real rose garden, and try some different varieties. So that summer when he visited back East, he took cuttings from four more roses in his aunt's garden, and six from his great aunt who lived in Rhode Island. On the train home, he met a man from St. Louis who had a garden, and after four hours of conversation, Charles decided to stop there. When he got off the train in Tulsa he had cuttings for forty-eight different roses.

This rose *(Gestures.)* is a rambler called "Red Cherokee," bred in 1913, the year Charles laid out a plan for his rose garden. There was an arbor on one end for the climbers, and a picket fence around it. Roses tend to be wild and unruly and a fence will help to contain their exuberance.

Charles planted all the roses that Fall, and in the Spring, every one came up. Virginia was six years old and Kenworthy was eleven. That same Spring, Rose Elizabeth announced her plan to make Kenworthy into a real Virginia gentleman. She was going to send him to the Virginia Military Institute. Little Virginia was grief-stricken. She prayed that something would happen to prevent her brother from going—maybe measles or chicken pox. But in September, Kenworthy went off to VMI.

He didn't like it there. He rebelled against all the rules, and drills and the hazing of the new plebes. He was reprimanded, docked, given demerits and confined to his room. He was sent to the guard house for throwing a glass of milk at a senior prefect who ordered him to lick the dust off his boots. Then in March, Kenworthy was expelled for unruly conduct and insubordination and he arrived back in Tulsa under a cloud of shame.

Every night at supper, Rose Elizabeth would say something about Southern manhood, and Kenworthy would refuse to let it pass. He would "talk back" in such a nasty tone that it brought tears to his mother's eyes. Then, instead of apologizing, he would throw down his knife and fork, push back from the table so hard his chair tipped over backwards, storm out and slam the door. Almost every night. Then Rose Elizabeth would sob and weep, and Charles and Virginia would go out to the garden. Charles built a bench under the arbor where Virginia could sit and read or draw while he weeded and pruned.

Before you plant the rose, it's a good thing to enrich the soil. Take equal parts of greensand, rock phosphate, bloodmeal, bone meal and humus. Add two parts of aged manure and then mix it all in with the dirt you dug out of the hole. *(Points to the wheelbarrow.)* These are actually refinements. You can leave everything out and the rose will grow anyway. In the old days they used to throw a fish head into the hole instead of bone meal, then add some manure. That's what my grandfather did.

By the time Virginia was ten years old, there were lots of bushes that were ten feet high. The American Beauty from Massachusetts was twelve feet. But Kenworthy was worse. He flew into rages even when his mother said nothing about being a Virginia gentleman. He yelled at her for talking behind his back, even though she wasn't saying a word.

One afternoon, he shouted at her and chased her up the stairs—he was a strong boy, sixteen years old. She ran into her room and locked the door and threw herself on the bed in hysterics. He broke the door down, and she ran, terrified, to the neighbors'. An ambulance came, with three attendants, and they finally found Ken in the garage. They put him in a strait-jacket and took him away.

Virginia got a red rash from her neck to her ankles. The doctor said it was hives and it might be caused by all the tension in the household.

Three weeks later, Ken came home from the hospital. At supper, Rose Elizabeth talked about how pretty the garden was looking—even though she never went out there because the sun could ruin her skin. Virginia's skin began to itch and get hot. Suddenly Ken shoved his plate on the floor and said his mother was trying to poison him. Then he ran out to the garage, locked himself in and set the garage on fire. That time, they took him to another hospital in another town.

Rose Elizabeth couldn't stand to visit him. Charles always took a bouquet of roses because Ken loved the smell and the colors.

Virginia's hives got terrible. She was sure that she was to blame for everything. One day she got up the nerve to ask her father if Ken would ever get well.

Charles told his daughter—she was twelve or thirteen by then—that Kenworthy was a paranoid schizophrenic, which most people call crazy. Virginia said she thought it was a punishment from God. Charles said no, he was pretty certain as a scientist and a gardener that it was something that's there in the plant all along but you can't see it at first. In a rose, it's called a "sport." You plant say a yellow rose and it grows true for a while—then, suddenly, it sports renegade shoots that bear maybe big pink blossoms instead of yellow, and if you cut them back, they grow in again thicker and stronger than ever. After a year or two the original plant has disappeared and the sport has taken over. Charles said that's what he thought had happened to Ken. Virginia said surely the whole process could be reversed, and Ken could return to his true self. Charles said it was a valid hypothesis, but he had never seen it happen in a rose.

Virginia never stopped praying that Ken would get well. No one knew about her burden. She seemed happy and normal. There were parties every week-end, and her dance card was always full.

When she was twenty-three, Virginia fell in love and got married—to my father, Tom. The day she got married, Virginia's hives went away. She and Tom bought a house on the block behind her parents. She could walk through her new back yard, cut through two vacant lots and be in her father's rose garden.

Virginia had two miscarriages. Rose Elizabeth said there was a curse in the blood, and it was wrong for her to even think of having children.

Virginia's hives came back. She would wake up in the night and have to go to the kitchen so Tom wouldn't hear her crying. Then she got pregnant again. After work, Charles would cut some fresh roses and go through to Virginia's back porch. They would sit on the glider and sip ice water.

The baby was born in the middle of August at three in the morning. When Charles got the call from Tom at the hospital, he went out to the garden and cut a huge bouquet of roses.

Tom and Virginia named the baby Charlotte in honor of Charles. That Fall, he took a new rose he had bred—a cross between the

American Beauty and a yellow rose from the man in St. Louis. He named this rose Charlotte in honor of his new granddaughter, and he planted it in late November when she was three months old.

The rose bloomed in May, a beautiful yellow-orange with a touch of pink in the center. A few weeks later, Charles came in early from the garden. He told Rose Elizabeth he felt tired and he was going to take a nap before supper. They said he must have just lain down when he had the heart attack.

In a few years the garden was overgrown. But many of the plants blossomed every Spring through the weeds, because roses are tenacious.

—So don't worry—when you have everything mixed up well, shovel some of the mix into the hole and make a small mound. Then unwrap the damp roots of the rose and spread them out over the soil on the mound. Add a little more soil around the roots to hold them in place. Add some more water, and work the roots in a little more. Then shovel on the rest of the soil, water it in well. And think about history. *(Blackout.)*

END OF PLAY

Donut Holes in Orbit

BY PRINCE GOMOLVILAS

FOR MY GRANDMOTHER

THE AUTHOR

Prince Gomolvilas is the author of *Big Hunk o' Burnin' Love, Seat Belts and Big Fat Buddhas,* and *The Theory of Everything.* His work has been produced by the Actors' Theatre (Santa Cruz), East West Players (Los Angeles) and Second Generation Productions (New York City). He has also developed plays at the Bay Area Playwrights Festival, The Lark Theatre Company, Ma-Yi Theatre Company, Mark Taper Forum, and South Coast Repertory. He received his MFA Degree in Playwriting from San Francisco State University, and he resides in San Francisco, the center of the universe.

ORIGINAL PRODUCTION

Donut Holes in Orbit was first produced at the Ensemble Studio Theatre, in Marathon '98, the 21st Annual Festival of One-Act Plays (Curt Dempster, Artistic Director; Jamie Richards, Executive Producer) in New York City in May, 1998. It was directed by Charles Karchmer with the following cast:

MRS. LEE . . . . Wai Ching Ho
ERIC . . . . Paul Whitthorne
ALICE . . . . Jina Oh
JOEY . . . . Barney Cheng

AUTHOR'S NOTE

Thank you, thank you, thank you: Robert C. Barker, Roy Conboy, Karen Folger Jacobs, and Brighde Mullins for being fabulous mentors; Curt Dempster, Jamie Richards, and everyone at EST for believing in my work; Barney, Jina, Paul, and Wai Ching for being born talented; and Charles Karchmer for being a damned good director. Many, many more people contributed to making this play a possibility, and I hope they know—even though they're not listed here—that they are greatly appreciated. And thanks to everyone who's ever attended one of my productions or readings, said a kind word to me, or wished me well.

CHARACTERS

(In order of speaking.)

MRS. LEE: forty-eight years old, a Chinese American, immigrated to America at the age of twenty-three

ERIC: twenty-six years old, a Caucasian American

ALICE: twenty-four years old, a Chinese American, born in the U.S.A.

JOEY: twenty-four years old, a Thai American, born in the U.S.A.

SETTING

Modesto, California

TIME

Present

SCENE I

A donut shop. Mrs. Lee behind the counter. Alice, Eric, and Joey in front. Joey leans on a mop.

MRS. LEE: I don't understand American donut. Big hole in the middle. Why big hole? No purpose, really. It doesn't make the donut look better. Or taste better. Or anything like that. Very sad for the donut. It's like some-body—how do you say—ripped out its soul. That's the word, right? Soul? Yes. Poor donut. Makes me feel so bad. So upset sometimes. Big empty hole where the soul should be.
(Pause.)

ERIC: Um: Mrs. Lee: donuts aren't alive; they don't have souls.

MRS. LEE: Oh, really? Thank you for figuring that out. Are you a detective? You must be a detective. Hah? Are you: are you Matlock? Hah? You Perry Mason? Hah?

ALICE: Mom, stop being so abrasive.

MRS. LEE: He talk to me like I'm crazy or something.

ERIC: I'm sorry; I didn't mean to offend.

ALICE: He's just making an observation.

MRS. LEE: You think I'm crazy, too?

ALICE: No.

MRS. LEE: You think I have Mad Cow Disease?

ERIC: I didn't mean anything by it.

MRS. LEE: Ai-yah. Young kids. Think they know it all. I'm just trying to tell you something.

ALICE: We know.

MRS. LEE: That's why you have to have respect.

ALICE: We *do* respect you.

MRS. LEE: No. Not respect for *me*.
(Pause.)

JOEY: For what then?
(Pause.)

MRS. LEE: Donut holes.
(Blackout.)

SCENE II

Alice stands, facing the audience.

ALICE: My mom. Believes. In aliens. The spaceship-flying, from-another-planet kind. She somehow got a hold of that *Communion* book—I think someone lent it to her. You know the book: the one with that picture on the cover: of that yellow alien creature with the big black bug eyes. It's supposedly a non-fiction account of one guy's encounters with "visitors." She read it cover to cover, and occasionally she would come to me and ask me things like what anal probes were. Anyway, the book scared the shit out of her. Slept with her bedroom light on for two months straight.

When Dad abandoned us six years ago, my mom and I knew he did it on his own volition. I mean, his leaving was so sudden and quiet and unexpected, but we knew he skipped town and flew back to Hong Kong. But for that first year or so, we didn't want to believe it so much that, even in public, my mom and I stood firmly by another version of what had happened:

The aliens got him.

(Blackout.)

SCENE III

An employee lunchroom. Alice and Eric at a table.

ERIC: Because why?
ALICE: Because I'm afraid.
ERIC: Of what?
ALICE: I don't wanna talk about it.
ERIC: Alice. C'mon. What are you afraid of?
    (Pause.)
ALICE: Of flying.
ERIC: What?!
ALICE: Flying.
ERIC: What do you mean you're afraid of flying?
ALICE: It means what it means.
ERIC: Are you telling me that's the reason?
ALICE: Yes.

ERIC: That's the sole reason you're not going?

ALICE: Yes.

ERIC: You're "afraid of flying."

ALICE: Yes, I am.

ERIC: That's absurd. There are ways around the phobia, Alice.

ALICE: I know that but—

ERIC: And besides which—"afraid of flying"—that's idiotic.

ALICE: It's not idiotic. Don't exaggerate, Eric.

ERIC: Oh. Please. Alice. First of all, I mean, Alice, c'mon: your father was a pilot.

ALICE: Not in America.

ERIC: Okay. In Hong Kong. When he was young. But that's just details. I'm just saying: don't you find it rather ironic that you're—so you say— afraid of flying?

ALICE: I don't wanna argue anymore.

ERIC: Who's arguing? We're discussing. This is a discussion. About our future. This is about our future together, Alice. Do we have a future together?

(Pause.)

ALICE: Do you love me?

ERIC: Do you love *me*?

ALICE: I asked you first.

ERIC: Well, I'm asking you now.

ALICE: I asked you first.

ERIC: And I'm asking you now.

(Pause.)

ALICE: All right. We'll answer the question at the same time.

ERIC: What do you mean?

ALICE: I'm gonna count to three. And on three we both say either yes or no in response to the question of whether or not we love each other. All right?

ERIC: That's got to be the most bizarre thing I've ever heard.

ALICE: Just do it, Eric.

ERIC: Okay, okay.

ALICE: Ready?

ERIC: Yes.

(Pause.)

ALICE: One. Two. Three.

(Neither of them say a thing. Blackout.)

SCENE IV

Donut shop. Mrs. Lee and Joey behind the counter.

MRS. LEE: Joey: I know you are not too smart. But that's okay. Some things you know. Like my daughter. Of course. You work in my shop since you were sixteen. Many years you know my daughter now. What? Eight years. Of course you know her well.

JOEY: I guess.

MRS. LEE: I want you to talk to her.

JOEY: Me?

MRS. LEE: Of course you! Who else am I talking to, hah? You think I'm talking to the donuts? Hah? Oh, yeah, sure, I'm talking to the donuts because I'm—what—Doctor Doolittle of Pastries?

JOEY: I wouldn't know.

MRS. LEE: Her company. You know her company?

JOEY: Corman Electronics?

MRS. LEE: Yes, Corman Electronics. They're shutting down their whole operation here in Modesto. Relocating to England. They want all employees to relocate, too. Everyone who goes will get big promotion and big pay raise.

JOEY: Is Alice going?

MRS. LEE: Ah-ha. Maybe you're not so dumb after all. Because this is our problem. She doesn't want to go. So good for her future, but she says she's not going.

JOEY: If going would be so good for her, why wouldn't she want to go?

MRS. LEE: She says she's afraid of flying. Stupid excuse. Maybe someone like you would believe her, but me: no way. I don't know what kind of game she's trying to play. She wants to stay in Modesto all her life or something? Hah? Is that any way to live?

JOEY: Maybe she likes it here.

MRS. LEE: Ai-yah. How do you say—get a grip. Modesto. That's where we are. Modesto: the Capital of Hell. Hmm. Nothing happens here.

JOEY: I guess you're right.

MRS. LEE: You, Joey, not a very good brain. But my daughter: so smart. Bright future. I don't want her to throw it all away. That's why you have to talk to her. Tell her that she should go.

JOEY: But why would she listen to me?

MRS. LEE: Very sorry to say this, breaks my heart to say this, but: you're the
only person she listens to.

JOEY: Why's that?

MRS. LEE: Ai-yah. If I knew that, it would be like knowing the meaning of
life.

JOEY: You don't know the meaning of life?

MRS. LEE: You think *you* know?

JOEY: Kind of.

MRS. LEE: You make me laugh so much sometimes. Okay. Mr. Philosophy.
What is the meaning of life?

(Pause.)

JOEY: Um. I forgot.

MRS. LEE: Ai-yah.

(Blackout.)

SCENE V

Joey stands, facing the audience.

JOEY: The summer right after I finished fourth grade was the summer somebody stole my glass eye.

    I was ten and, um, very used to the other kids avoiding me and call-
ing me Chinaman even though my parents are from Thailand and I was
born in California. But I wanted everyone to like me, and I don't know
why everybody thought this was neat but I could—it's true—I could
take out my glass eye. I mean, just pull it right from the socket and hold
it in my hand. And any time I'd pop that thing out, a bunch of kids
would gather around me and just be totally amazed.

    One day some kid snatched the eye right out of my hand, took off,
and sold it to a pawn shop.

    I went to the shop, and the guy there wouldn't give me my eye back.
It would cost me twenty dollars, he said. I had my life savings in my
pocket, but all *it* added up to was ninety-seven cents. Now that money
did buy me an eye patch which I wore all the way home to cover up the
big hole in my face where my eye shoulda been.

    I knew my dad would hit me if he found out that I lost my glass
eye, so I told him I needed the patch because I was Captain Hook. And
I thought I could keep that thing on until I was eighteen and moved out.

Surprisingly, my parents let me wear the patch for the rest of day and even let me go to sleep with it. But my dad said it had to come off in the morning.

In my room, I cried at the thought of what would happen when Dad found out. I couldn't go to sleep; just laid there crying.

Sometime in the middle of the night, my dad came into my room while I kept my eye half closed so he would think I was sleeping. He put something on the night stand and left the room. When I flicked on the light, I saw my glass eye on that little table, staring right at me.

I don't know how he found out or how he got my eye back or why he didn't lay a hand on me. But I thought it was so great that my dad did that for me. And I thought that maybe things would be different now.

But the thing is:

After that night:

I never saw him again.

(Blackout.)

SCENE VI

A park. Alice and Joey play catch.

ALICE: Why are you so concerned?

JOEY: Because.

ALICE: I'm not going, Joey.

JOEY: It'd be so great for you. To get away.

ALICE: You want me to go?

JOEY: No...I mean...I'm...I don't know. You've always had a thing for England. All those books and photographs. Ever since I met you, it's like you love the place, even though you've never been there.

ALICE: Why are you making such a big deal out of it?

JOEY: I don't know. Because...uh...well...God. I can't do this right. I can't.

ALICE: What?

(Pause.)

JOEY: Your mother got me to do this.

ALICE: What?!

JOEY: Sorry.

ALICE: My mother put you up to this?

JOEY: Yeah.

ALICE: I can't believe her.

JOEY: I'm sorry, Alice. She scares me.

ALICE: She's so devious.

JOEY: I mean, just when I think of her, I get goose bumps. Eeeee.

ALICE: I can't fly, Joey. It's that simple.

JOEY: I know.

ALICE: It's like how you feel about my mom; that's how I feel about going up in the air.

(Pause.)

JOEY: I was watching this talk show the other day—I forget which one; I watch all of them almost, with my mom—and they were talking about when you're afraid of flying, and this was kinda interesting: do you ever have dreams that you're falling?

ALICE: What do you mean?

JOEY: Well, they were saying that—it was Montel Williams; that's who it was. He wrote that book about himself called *Mountain, Get Out of My Way.*

ALICE: *(Laughing.)* You've got to be kidding me.

JOEY: What?

ALICE: That's the name of his book?

JOEY: Yeah. But anyway they were saying that people who have a fear of flying sometimes have dreams that they're falling. And that these dreams and that fear are linked, related somehow. So I mean, do you have dreams that you're falling?

ALICE: No. I don't know.

JOEY: You don't know?

ALICE: I don't remember them.

JOEY: You don't?

ALICE: I don't think I have them.

JOEY: Them?

ALICE: Dreams.

JOEY: You don't think you have dreams about falling?

ALICE: No, no, no. I don't think I have dreams, period.

JOEY: Wait a minute.

ALICE: I don't think I dream.

JOEY: Of course you do. Everybody dreams.

ALICE: Well, I don't.

(Pause.)

JOEY: Hold on. But what about the journals?

(Pause.)

ALICE: I didn't want to tell you.

JOEY: I don't understand.

ALICE: I haven't written in them.

JOEY: You haven't written in any of the dream journals?

ALICE: No.

JOEY: But I've been giving you one every year for Christmas.

ALICE: I know. I have eight empty dream journals under my bed.

JOEY: Why didn't you tell me?

ALICE: I didn't wanna hurt your feelings.

   (Pause.)

JOEY: I feel so stupid.

ALICE: Joey.

JOEY: Every year. A new journal. And you don't even use them.

ALICE: I think they're great though. They really are.

JOEY: They're just collecting dust.

ALICE: I wish I could write in them. But what can I do?

JOEY: Nothing, I guess.

ALICE: Nothing.

JOEY: Nothing.

   (Pause.)

ALICE: What?

   (Pause.)

JOEY: Nothing.

   (Blackout.)

SCENE VII

Donut shop. Mrs. Lee behind the counter. Eric in front.

MRS. LEE: What kind of boyfriend are you?

ERIC: What do you mean?

MRS. LEE: Three years.

ERIC: I know.

MRS. LEE: Don't you think that's a long time?

ERIC: I guess.

MRS. LEE: And you act so surprised that she doesn't want to go to England with you.

ERIC: What do you mean? She says she's afraid of flying.

MRS. LEE: That's so stupid that it can't be the reason. You're not dumb enough to believe it, are you?

ERIC: I guess not.

MRS. LEE: You guess not. You guess all the time. Oh. What? What kind of jeans you wear? Guess Jeans? Hah? You wear Guess Jeans? Hah?

ERIC: What are you getting at?

MRS. LEE: You don't show her that you care about her.

ERIC: How's that?

MRS. LEE: Ai-yah. Why is every boy in Modesto so stupid?

ERIC: What?

MRS. LEE: England is a long way to go. You need to let her know that once she gets there that you won't abandon her, leave her alone.

ERIC: I wouldn't leave her.

MRS. LEE: But she doesn't *know* that. She needs a guarantee. You know what I'm talking about?

ERIC: Ah. I think I know what you're saying.

MRS. LEE: Do it quick before it's too late. Go to Vegas. They have a Drive-Thru Chapel of Love. Very easy. Very convenient. Don't even have to get out of your car.

ERIC: I didn't think it would have to come down to this.

MRS. LEE: Down to what?

ERIC: Marriage.

MRS. LEE: Oh. And you think *I* jump for joy that she chose you? White boy. You want me to buy you a hamburger?

ERIC: I don't understand what you're saying.

MRS. LEE: I'm saying: respect. You have to respect marriage. Respect love. Didn't your mom and dad ever tell you about the facts of life? The bees and the birds?

ERIC: I wasn't home during that lecture.

MRS. LEE: Mmm-hmm. American kids. You see? Don't respect their parents.

ERIC: They didn't respect *me,* either.

MRS. LEE: And you think that's *their* fault?

ERIC: I don't know. I guess.

MRS. LEE: There you go again. You guess, you guess. Ai-yah. Get out of my store, and do what I'm telling you, if you know what's best for your life.

ERIC: All right. Thanks a lot for the—

MRS. LEE: Get out of my store!

(Eric exits. Blackout.)

SCENE VIII

Eric stands, facing the audience.

ERIC: My father—when he was still living with my family—one time told me that relationships are assignments. Everybody you come into contact with, be it a stranger, a relative, or a lover, is a test. The universe, God, the divine intelligence of the world—whatever the fuck you want to call it—thrusts people upon us because these people that come into our lives represent lessons we need to learn. They are the exams of our souls.

I cheated throughout high school.

I was a pro; never got caught. Crib sheets, looking over shoulders, answers written on my wrist. I faked my way through academia, and I was rewarded with a diploma.

And getting away with deceit so many times has got me thinking that lying and conniving is the way to get me what I want. And right now I want Alice. I want Alice because I don't want to be lonely. Loneliness scares me more than death.

I don't know what we've got between us, and it may very well be nothing, but at least it resembles something, and that's important to me.

But if what my father said was true, if God exists, how the hell do I cheat here? Because like in that Bette Midler song, right? "God is watching us."

But that high school cockiness hasn't really subsided any, and I think there's got to be a way to escape His gaze. And I've figured that there *is* because there must be moments, there must be short instances:

When God...blinks.

(Blackout.)

SCENE IX

A front porch. Alice and Joey sit.

ALICE: Don't give me the cold shoulder, Joey. I mean, I didn't set out to hurt your feelings, you know. I would never do that. You mean too much to me.
(Pause.)
JOEY: I do?
(Pause.)

ALICE: You're the only friend I've got in this God-awful town.
> (*Pause.*)

JOEY: You're the only friend I've got, too.
> (*Pause.*)

ALICE: So am I forgiven?
> (*Pause.*)

JOEY: Of course. I could never be mad at you for too long anyway even when
> I should be.
> (*Pause.*)

ALICE: Why's that?
> (*Pause.*)

JOEY: Because I'm in love with you.
> (*Pause. Blackout.*)

SCENE X

Employee lunchroom. Alice and Eric at a table.

ALICE: You've got to be kidding me
ERIC: No, I'm not.
ALICE: Where's the ring?
ERIC: Huh?
ALICE: Where's the ring then?
ERIC: What ring?
ALICE: You're pathetic.
ERIC: I thought we could pick it out together.
ALICE: I know why you're doing this.
ERIC: No, you don't.
ALICE: Yes, I do.
ERIC: No, you don't.
ALICE: Yes, I do.
ERIC: You don't.
ALICE: I do.
ERIC: You do not.
ALICE: My mother put you up to this.

(Pause.)
ERIC: Okay, so you do.
(Blackout.)

SCENE XI

Mrs. Lee stands, facing the audience.

MRS. LEE: Confession time. I must confess because I had a very scary dream about little yellow creatures who came into my bedroom and were pinching my skin. Pinching me in order to get me to tell the whole truth.

I am a selfish woman.

I want to send my daughter away to England, not because it will be good for *her* future, but because it would be good for *my* future. I want her to make a lot of money, so she can send it to me. So I can put it in my bank account. And maybe I will someday have enough to go back to Hong Kong. Where I belong.

I gave this country a chance. I gave it many chances. Wah. Land of Opportunity. Gave me nothing. Just a donut shop and a broken heart. Wake up every morning, seven days a week, very early, to sell people donuts. Then go home to an empty bed. That's all.

Ai-yah. America. I work hard for you. I love you. I even become a citizen. Took a test and everything. And I thought I belong here. But people still look at me funny when I talk to them.

My husband had an even worse time than me. I guess that's why he left.

He owned this shop with me, you know. But now it's all mine. Finally paid off all loans. And it's mine. But I don't want it anymore.

All I have left is Alice. And look at her. All grown up. Don't need me anymore. Neither does America. But I don't have enough money to go back and live in Hong Kong. Believe it or not, donuts are not a booming business. So what I do? Wait for a miracle to happen? Wait for my daughter to become a millionaire? Give me some answers, America. Give me some help. I beg you, U.S.A., let me go home.

Let me go home.
(Blackout.)

SCENE XII

Front porch. Alice and Joey sit.

JOEY: Ever since I met you.

ALICE: That long?

JOEY: I just never had the guts to say anything.
  (Pause.)

ALICE: It's gonna hurt to hear this.
  (Pause.)

JOEY: I'm an adult.
  (Pause.)

ALICE: I don't love you in *that* way, Joey. I mean, you're my best friend and everything, and I *do* love you, but not like that.
  (Pause.)

JOEY: You gonna marry Eric?

ALICE: No. No, I'm not. He's not the right person for me.

JOEY: And I'm not either, huh?

ALICE: No. No, you're not.
  (Pause.)

JOEY: Do you think you'll ever be able to love me in *that* way?
  (Pause.)

ALICE: No. *(Pause.)* You okay? *(Pause.)* Joey? *(Pause.)* You okay? *(Pause.)* Joey?
  (Blackout.)

SCENE XIII

Employee lunchroom. Alice and Eric at a table.

ERIC: Why not?

ALICE: Because I don't love you.
  (Pause.)

ERIC: Well, I don't love you, either.
  (Pause.)

ALICE: So what does this mean?

ERIC: I don't know that it means anything.

ALICE: What are you talking about?

ERIC: I mean, the ring's bought and paid for.

ALICE: Are you crazy? You still wanna get married?

ERIC: Yeah. Why not?

ALICE: We don't love each other, Eric.

ERIC: That didn't stop my mom and my dad. Doesn't stop most people.

ALICE: Well, I'm not most people. You think I'm just gonna throw my life away?

ERIC: You haven't already?

ALICE: What the hell is that supposed to mean?

ERIC: It means that I know you're not afraid of flying.

ALICE: Yes, I am.

ERIC: You don't want to go to London because you hate this job.

ALICE: No, I don't.

ERIC: C'mon, Alice. Straight out of high school you went through two years of community college and ended up here. Working for this goddamn company. Four years and what? No pay raise. No promotions. No pat on the back, even. Same thing, day in, day out. *(Pause.)* When you were young, you didn't dream about being here.

ALICE: So what?

ERIC: So I don't know what I'm saying. I'm just: when you were a kid, what were your dreams?

ALICE: What?

ERIC: What were your dreams?

ALICE: I don't remember.

ERIC: Don't be embarrassed. I mean, hell, *I* didn't dream about doing *this*. Nobody did. I mean, I watch these other employees: some of 'em been here twenty, thirty years, miserable, and I'm *scared*. Is *that* what I have to look forward to? *(Pause.)* But you know what scares me even more?

ALICE: What?

ERIC: That I'll turn out like my dad. Barely able to support himself, let alone our entire family. Two factory jobs wasn't enough. He was so ashamed of himself that he eventually couldn't take it anymore and left our family. *(Pause.)* Yeah, I hate this shit job, but once we're in London, our salary's gonna get bumped up to a point that all of this shit'll be tolerable. I'm sorry to say that my future, my security, rests on how much money I can save, but that's all that matters. My dreams don't anymore. *(Pause.)* I'm still at this company for the same reason you are.

ALICE: Are you?

ERIC: And for the same reason we've been together for three years.

ALICE: And why's that?

(Pause.)

ERIC: We're afraid.
(*Blackout.*)

SCENE XIV

Alice stands, facing the audience.

ALICE: My dad used to be a home movie enthusiast. He had one of those archaic Super-8 cameras, and he would film just about everything whenever he got the chance to. I mean, *everything,* and it embarrassed Mom and me. He would film trips to the zoo, parties, dinners at restaurants, standing in line at the DMV.

I guess that's where my desire to become a filmmaker began. With my dad. So I guess it's really ironic that that's where the desire ended too. With my dad.

Because when you're told enough times that you're not good enough to do that, you begin to believe it.

I wanted to go to film school, you know. Quite adamant about it, in fact. He saw that I wasn't gonna listen to him. That I was gonna become a failure. Just like him. So he gave up. Left town. Split. Disappeared in the middle of the night. No note. Nothing.

So I decided to stay in Modesto. With my mother.

And I know it's really cheezy and pathetic and melodramatic to talk about pieces of broken heart, but that's the only thing that comes into my mind when I think about how I feel. Both my mom and I had shattered pieces all over. And we've been trying to put them back in place for years. But the longer and harder we try, the more I realize that I've picked up some of hers and she's picked up some of mine.
(*Blackout.*)

SCENE XV

Donut shop. Mrs. Lee holds four envelopes. Alice stands nearby.

ALICE: What were you doing in my room?
MRS. LEE: I was cleaning it.
ALICE: You shouldn't be in my room.

MRS. LEE: *(Of the envelopes.)* Why didn't you tell me about these?

ALICE: It didn't matter.

MRS. LEE: *(Reading.)* "The London International Film School."

ALICE: Yeah.

MRS. LEE: You got in. Four years in a row you got in, and they offer you a scholarship. Why didn't you tell me? Why didn't you go?

ALICE: I don't know.

(Pause.)

MRS. LEE: Flying? Is that really it? No problem, Alice. Many different things to help you fly. Pills. Hypnotists. And acupuncture: yes, it's true. I read about acupuncture. I bet I could even do it on you. How hard can it be? Go to the store. Buy a few needles. Very simple. Many different ways to help you fly.

(Pause.)

ALICE: But if I go: what's going to happen to you?

MRS. LEE: Ai-yah. I'm a grown woman.

ALICE: Because it's not just about me, you know. This is gonna affect you, too. I mean, going to school, I wouldn't be making any money at all. I won't have anything to give you. Your savings account's just gonna sit there.

MRS. LEE: Then let it sit. It needs a rest anyway.

ALICE: But...England...it's so far away.

(Pause. Mrs. Lee leads Alice outside.)

MRS. LEE: Alice. You are standing here on this porch. Out there, what do you see?

ALICE: What do you mean?

MRS. LEE: Use your eyes. As far as you can see. What is it?

ALICE: Um...the horizon?

MRS. LEE: And what's beyond the horizon?

ALICE: Um, the sea.

MRS. LEE: And what's beyond that?

ALICE: The...sky...and the sun.

MRS. LEE: And beyond that?

ALICE: The stars and space.

MRS. LEE: And after that?

ALICE: After that? I don't know. More space, stretching out to infinity.

MRS. LEE: Right. Now look above you. What do you see?

ALICE: The blue sky and the sun.

MRS. LEE: And what's beyond that?

ALICE: Space...all the way to infinity.

MRS. LEE: So wherever you turn and look, whichever direction you point your eyes, what's way out there?

ALICE: Space, stretching to infinity.

MRS. LEE: The same space, all going to infinity. So you see?

ALICE: What?

MRS. LEE: That makes you the center of the universe. Wherever you go, whichever state or country you're in, is the same space, stretching to the same infinity. So you see? Every point in the universe is the same point. Wherever you are, you are always the center of the universe. So am I. No matter how far apart we are, we are both at the same point in the universe: the exact center.

ALICE: I don't think I understand what you're saying. And I'm not so sure *you* understand what you're saying. Sounds like something out of one of your new age books.

MRS. LEE: It is. But *I* know what I mean.

ALICE: What?

(Pause. Mrs. Lee hands the envelopes to Alice. Pause.)

MRS. LEE: Go. Alice. Your life is waiting for you.

(Blackout.)

SCENE XVI

Front porch. Alice and Joey stand. Two suitcases and two carry-ons on the ground.

JOEY: Well. I guess this is it.

ALICE: Yeah. I've got the Dramamine in my pocket. Got three small paper bags in my purse. I'm ready to vomit.

JOEY: You'll be fine.

ALICE: Hope so.

(Pause.)

JOEY: Alice. I wanted to say, um, that you've...uh...been a really important part of my life, you know. I don't know if you know that or believe it, but it's true. I mean, I've lived in Modesto all my life, and I'm pretty much gonna die here, and everything here's so...the *same,* you know what I'm saying? I always know what's gonna happen every day, and it can be pretty boring. *(Pause.)* But out of all those predictable things that I can expect to see every day, I...always look forward to seeing you. I really do. *(Pause.)* And I understand what we talked about, and I understand how you feel and everything, and I just want you to know that I don't hold it against you or anything, and I don't know, I'm rambling, and I guess this is just my way of saying that I'm really gonna miss you. Alice. I'm gonna miss you a lot.

ALICE: Joey, I'm gonna miss you, too. I'm only gonna be gone for three years, and that's not that long. And I'll write, and I'm coming back to visit as much as I can.

JOEY: But it won't be the same.

ALICE: No, it won't.

JOEY: Um. It:

(Pause.)

ALICE: What?

JOEY: No. It's stupid.

ALICE: What is it?

(Pause.)

JOEY: It hurts.

(Pause. Alice embraces Joey. Pause. They let go.)

JOEY: I'm gonna split.

ALICE: All right.

(Joey starts heading off.)

ALICE: Oh, wait a minute, Joey?

JOEY: What?

ALICE: I can't believe I almost forgot to tell you.

JOEY: What?

ALICE: I wrote my very first entry in my dream journal this morning.

JOEY: You did?

ALICE: Yes.

JOEY: You wrote in the dream journal?

ALICE: Yes.

JOEY: You mean you had a dream last night?

ALICE: Yes. I remember it. I remember my dream.

JOEY: What was it?

(Pause.)

ALICE: It was my father.

JOEY: You dreamt about your father?

ALICE: Yeah. He was standing in this green field, and he had his back turned towards me. But somehow he felt my presence, and he turned around, and his eyes were so lucid like he could see into my soul or something, and he talked to me.

JOEY: He did?

ALICE: Yeah.

JOEY: What'd he say?

(*Pause.*)

ALICE: He said: (*Pause.*) "Alice." (*Pause.*) "Fly."

(*Pause. Fade to black.*)

END OF PLAY

The Jade Mountain

BY DAVID MAMET

THE AUTHOR

David Mamet (Playwright) is the author of the plays *Oleanna, Glengarry Glen Ross* (1984 Pulitzer Prize and New York Drama Critics Circle Award), *American Buffalo, The Old Neighborhood, A Life In The Theater, Speed The Plow, Edmond, Lakeboat, The Water Engine, The Woods, Sexual Perversity In Chicago, Reunion* and *The Cryptogram* (1995 Obie Award). His translations and adaptations include *Red River* by Pierre Laville and *The Cherry Orchard, Three Sisters* and *Uncle Vanya* by Anton Chekov. His films include *The Postman Always Rings Twice, The Verdict, The Untouchables, House Of Games* (writer/director), *Oleanna* (writer/director), *Homicide* (writer/director), *The Spanish Prisoner* (writer/director), *Hoffa, The Edge,* and *Wag The Dog.* Mr. Mamet is also the author of *Warm And Cold,* a book for children with drawings by Donald Sultan, and two other children's books, *Passover* and *The Duck And The Goat; Writing In Restaurants, Some Freaks,* and *Make-Believe Town,* three volumes of essays; *The Hero Pony,* a book of poems; *Three Children's Plays, On Directing Film, The Cabin, True And False,* and the novel *The Village.* His most recent books include a new novel, *The Old Religion,* and an acting book, *True & False.*

ORIGINAL PRODUCTION

The Jade Mountain was first produced at the Ensemble Studio Theatre, in Marathon '98, the 21st Annual Festival of One-Act Plays (Curt Dempster, Artistic Director; Jamie Richards, Executive Producer) in New York City in May, 1998. It was directed by Curt Dempster with the following cast:

A. . . . . James Murtaugh
B . . . . Chris Ceraso

Two Men.

A: When the monkeys come up. But we didn't know what they were. We thought we were under attack. On the next day when it cleared, we were above the clouds. Most of the time. But it cleared, we were above the clouds. Most of the time. But it socked in, and when it cleared, back in Wisconsin, often you would wait, sometimes into the afternoon, 'til it burned off, but usually by ten or nine or by eleven anyway, one time I doused this balsa wood airplane. With lighter fluid, and put a string on it, and lighted the string. And threw it. By the Lake. And I felt guilty for it. Do you know, though I do not know why, unless it was that I was plain' with *fire;* yes, I think that is what it is, but the *curious* thing is that I should feel *guilty,* you know, when it never did ignite.

B: It didn't catch?

A: No.

B: The plane.

A: No. It didn't.

B: Did you soak the string?

A: The string.

B: The lighter fluid?

A: As I *spoke* I thought that you were gone' to ask me. And my first thought was "of course," but, as I think on it, I think how could I have, as it did not ignite, and subsequently, perhaps, that was the cause of my—it's not astonishment—of my *surprise* when it didn't catch.

B: Could the wind have blown it out?

A: ...but up above the clouds. *(Pause.)* Also. On our Observation Post. There was a *cave,* and it was naturally occurring. As I b'lieve they are. You hear "a manmade cave"...you hear "A natural cave"...which is it that you hear?

B: "A natural cave."

A: Yes. And "A manmade cave." But I think that you hear "a natural cave." When, *why* would you hear that, as I think *all* caves are natural? I was going to say, "All caves are natural except those that're *man*made." But I think you hear "a natural cave," and I think *all* caves are natural, for, if not, what are they? But holes in the earth. In a "hill," I suppose. They would have to be, and it *is* possible the wind blew it out; but, if so, then we're back to that same question of if I had gone and soaked it in the gasoline, and, if not, *why* not. For could I not of known that if I did *not* the wind would blow it out, and further, perhaps I *desired* that the plane would not catch, what do you think; and *if* that is the case, that I *contrived* it not to burn, then why would I feel guilty?

You could look back and say "what a child—to have devised a scheme to *be* and *not* be that thing which he wished both to be and not to be.

B: And what was that?

A: I want to say "a mischief maker," but I think that's not the thing.

B: What is the thing? *(Pause.)* What is the thing, then?

A: A man.

B: He wished to be a man.

A: I think that is what it is, and I still haven't told you about the Etruscan Statue. In *breaking* a thing, a rule, a way-of-being, perhaps.

B: To become a man. By doing that.

A: I think so. But then why would I feel guilty? Anyways. We thought that we were under attack. And we heard this *chattering. (Pause.)* Humans talking. Humans talking. Why would they, why would they *talk* so loud, you'd say, if they were trying to avoid detection. I don't know. Do you know, several times in my life. I have heard ghosts. And it's a common story. In Wisconsin. Up near the Northern Peninsula. In the North. I think there's something fitting about that. Do you?

B: I don't know.

A: And it seems there is and I think there are plots of land. Which exude things. *(Pause.)* I don't think that we create them there. I think they *live* there. I think they live there. There were ghosts. Several times. I could describe them to you.

B: What were they?

A: Well, they were noises. On the edge of sleep, you'd hear them. Or reading a book. When your thoughts…

B: …when your thoughts were elsewhere.

A: That's right. People talking. Talking low. "What is that out there?" Seldom when there was anyone there. In the trailer. Who you could say. Who you could look to, not even for, for *comfort.*

B: What is wrong with comfort?

A: …but, later, to say, "Wasn't that real? What *was* that? That 'talking'." There was no one there. There was nobody there. How could there have been? In the woods. And what would they, why had they come there. In the middle of the night?

B: To do you harm.

A: I can't say so. Then why was I frightened? Do you know? And *at the time.*

(Pause.) Once I took a gun to see. I started out the door. As I went out the door, I said, "I do not want to know." And, I'll tell you: I said to myself at the time, "Are you *content*. To spend the rest of your life *knowing* that you lacked the strength. To go out that door." And I said, if the test is to go out that door, or to stay, then I am going to stay.

B: And are you content?

A: No. I never was content.

(Pause.)

B: Would you like a cup of tea?

A: Yes. I would.

(B gestures off.)

B: Are you tired?

A: Yes. I am. What is contentment, *finally,* I don't know, but *'enough',* when you have been deprived, perhaps, do you think?

B: I don't know.

A: But that could be one of the definitions.

B: Yes. Certainly.

A: Couldn't it?

B: Yes. It could.

A: When I looked at the *rock. (Pause.)* I had pictures of it somewhere. Where have they gone? Funny, that the things which mean something to *me,* what can they mean to *you?* Finally. What can they mean. Nothing, really. Things that happened. If I told you. Once in a museum. Six men. Schemed for a week. To remove a priceless artifact. Beyond price. And what happened to it. Or the mountain. Things that made us. What we are. After all the shit of this world. And all philosophy. And thought. And religion. And literature. What makes us, then, but a rest. When we are tired, or warmth. When we are cold. A release of some sort. Friendship, maybe, then, is just we know that they aren't going to kill us. But we had to go through it. *Don't* we? Can you *doubt* it? To come out again? *(Pause.)* Then why do I feel so guilty...

(C brings in tea things and departs.)

A: ...over it? But when they tried to hit the rock they could not hit it. We had *no* ricochets in the cave. *No* rounds. *Nothing.* All of it outside. *(Pause.)* Outside. On the rock. And we *lay* on it. And peppered the trail. At will. For it ran into China. And if we found them on it, they were either going *in* or coming *out.* Either way. Well, good. They're gonna play "catch up"? Now, I can't blame 'em. But you aren't going to get *in* there. I think someone took 'em on the Hospital Ship. Do you know, you never meet a guy but that some buddy, or hear "heard" of someone won two hundred thousand dollars coming back, a poker game, a crap game, something—but I do not think it's true. Do you see, those are the *true* stories of the Supernatural. *(Of tea.)* There's nothing in this.

B: What do you mean?

(Pause.)

A: There's nothing in this.

B: Of what sort? Is that a question? *(Pause.)* What would there be in it? *(Pause.)* In the cup. Do you mean?

A: Perhaps if I drank it I'd have a dream. Did you ever think that? That you would be released, or that you been poisoned? Many thought that.

B: ...they did...

A: Yes. That someone had *adulterated* a drink. And it never was *food,* do you know? But a drink. And it made them crazy.

B: ...that someone had put something in their drink.

A: But I said coffee itself was sufficient.

B: To?

A: To *warp* you. To speed you up. So *thoroughly* you never would come home. Let alone... *(Sighs.)* And, in Olden Days. I would blow half a pack of Camels in the last ten miles of a march. Meant *nothing* to me. On Deck. On the Med cruise, bet against our man, did fifteen hundred pushups, perhaps. I *myself* did five, six hundred. It was *nothing.* And the coffee, I think, burned, or irritated me. Or something. To the point I had grown *old.* And I can't do it. *(Pause.)* No. I can't do it. The foods that I ate. The deeds I did. *(Pause.)* "Behave appropriately, then." you might say. But I don't know. It's a shithole. Isn't it?

Praying for some, some, something to lift, then, you say, "I'm happy now." When you remember *life* was when you didn't think about it, and that's all it was.

B: But isn't that a part of?

A: Fuck you, then. Were you *there?* You cannot *begin* to imagine. What we did. Where we *were*...what we *did*...For I tell you. *(Pause.)* A mountain made of Jade. Carved figures. Hewn from it. Of the *Buddha*...and, acrost, of the Blessed Virgin, and such Gold, that if we took one chalice. Or bowl, each of us, would be beyond, *beyond* fabulous wealth. *Beyond, beyond* the Etruscan Statue. Encrusted with Jewels. As they lay there. *(Pause.)* But we took nothing.

The essence of it was the Guard. But if he was so ineffective could that be his people, you see, this is what concerned me, in the time that past, had wanted to invite rather than to dissuade us. From going in.

B: I believe we have to move on.

A: Also, could you not, however, say the same of any temptation?

B: Of course you could.

A: Someone said "the vase will free us." I don't think so. For how many times were we not possessed of that thing we thought was the talisman, only to have it shatter, some sort? That guy on the deck. When the ship was "et up" with our bloke did the fifteen hundred, and they welshed on up, the vase, that dropped off his lap, getting from the car. The one round that entered that cave. On the Hospital Ship. Some guy, Huh. *You* wouldn't know him. His spine severed. Shit, you say, I'd rather be screaming than drugged. But that's not the case—and at the *end* I must say that the voices were those I would wrong. In later life, for I can not, for the *life* of me, give you another reading of who in the world they could be. And what they were striving to tell me. *(Pause.)* *Why* did the plane not burn?

B: The point not that it did not burn, but you were guilty as you did not wish it to.

A: Is that the case? Is that the thing of it, then? Is that what you came to tell me? *(Pause.)* Well. *(Pause.)* Well, that's not nothing. *(Pause.)* And if they *had* transpired, then we would not be here today. Isn't that true? *(Pause.)*

B: Yes. That's true.

A: And we have to move on…

B: Yes.

A: Well, then. *(Pause.)* Well, then. *(Pause.)* Then, let's do that, then.

END OF PLAY

Scrapple

BY JENNIFER MATTERN

scrap•ple (skrap´ əl) *n.* cornmeal boiled with scraps of pork
and allowed to set, then sliced and fried.

—Webster's New World College Dictionary,
Third Edition

FOR ED BAKER (AND HIS BASEBALL CAP)

THE AUTHOR

Jennifer Mattern was born and raised in Philadelphia. She graduated from Grinnell College in 1992 before leaving for Sátoraljaújhely, Hungary, where she taught English and Drama at a small high school. In 1997 she received an MFA in Theatre (Acting/Playwriting) from Sarah Lawrence College, where several of her plays were produced, including *Blue Doesn't Mean Anything, Just Resting* and *The Barracuda and Mister Fish*. Mattern has acted in numerous productions in Minneapolis and New York, including Judith Thompson's *Lion in the Streets* (Isobel), Edward Allan Baker's *Rosemary with Ginger* (Ginger), and Arthur Giron's *Edith Stein* (title role). She currently resides in New York City.

ORIGINAL PRODUCTION

Scrapple was first produced at the Ensemble Studio Theatre, in Marathon '98, the 21st Annual Festival of One-Act Plays (Curt Dempster, Artistic Director; Jamie Richards, Executive Producer) in New York City, May, 1998. It was directed by Susann Brinkley with the following cast:

JACK. . . . . William Wise
ANNIE . . . . Molly Price

CHARACTERS

JACK: late fifties
ANNIE: Jack's daughter, late twenties to early thirties

SETTING

The shabby kitchen of a Philadelphia rowhouse

TIME

2:15 AM, a night in early September

Jack sits at a cherry-wood table doing a crossword puzzle and smoking Marlboros. Occasionally he coughs, rubs his chest and looks up at the clock. He is listening to an oldies' station which is currently playing "Under the Boardwalk." Annie, his daughter, sits outside on the back stoop, unseen and unheard by Jack. Annie wears an unattractive bridesmaid dress and a denim jacket, and she holds a drooping bouquet of flowers. She is overweight, awkward. She studies a photograph in her hand. After a beat or two, she stuffs the photograph into a ratty evening bag, rises and enters the kitchen through the back door.

JACK: Huh. Look at you.

ANNIE: Yeah.

JACK: Jesus. Nice flowers. What, they pick em off the graves behind the church?

ANNIE: Whatever that means. Why are you up anyway?

JACK: Christ, how much you pay for that thing? *(Pause.)* The dress.
(Annie does not respond.)

JACK: You had to pay for it, right? They don't buy it?

ANNIE: Right.

JACK: Christ. That don't seem right somehow to me. I don't know. *(Pause.)* They feed you good, though?

ANNIE: Pretty good. *(Pause.)* They had deviled eggs.

JACK: Eggs. Christ. Went all out.

ANNIE: It wasn't just eggs.

JACK: Oh, it wasn't. What. Oatmeal.

ANNIE: Meat.

JACK: Oh. Meat.

ANNIE: Beef. They had all kinds of, you know, beef.

JACK: How many kinds of beef can you have?

ANNIE: You know what I mean. The ham or the roast beef, whatever, with the guys in the chef hats slicing it for you. *(Pause.)* It was nice.

JACK: Uh huh. So speaking of nice, what was it, a hundred bucks? Your dress—

ANNIE: About.

JACK: Don't tell me you paid more than a hundred bucks for that thing.

ANNIE: We all did, that's just what you do. I had to.

JACK: Had to my ass. You didn't have to do anything.

ANNIE: I'm going to bed, goodnight.

JACK: Aw come on. Annie. You hungry?

ANNIE: No.

JACK: Aw come on, you can't tell me eggs at six filled you up. I know how you eat.

ANNIE: I told you, they had all kinds of other stuff—

JACK: Right, meat from the wandering butchers.

ANNIE: They weren't *wandering*. They had their own little, you know, station.

JACK: Aw, now that's funny. I pictured two of them carrying around a dead pig tied to a stick while a third guy hacked off a pork chop for somebody here at this table, a pork butt for somebody there at that table…

ANNIE: *(Laughing in spite of herself.)* Get out of here, you're crazy.

JACK: I can't remember the last time I went to a wedding. Wait a sec, sit down for a minute and help me with a couple of these. Take a look at, uh, seventy-two down and I'll make us some scrapple.
(Annie sits and stares listlessly at the crossword puzzle as Jack gets the block of scrapple from the refrigerator.)

ANNIE: I'm not hungry.

JACK: Somebody else might believe that one, but I know how you like to eat. Christ, all you wanted to do when you were eight or nine was go to Ponderosa. It was 'Daddy, Daddy, take me to Ponderosa!' every other night.

ANNIE: Please.

JACK: You ate everybody under the table. One time I got you an twenty-ounce T-bone steak, bloody like you liked it, just to see if you could do it.

ANNIE: Disgusting. Like I was a dog.

JACK: You ate the whole goddamn thing and you were still hungry for more! Went around the table begging for everybody else's scraps. Sucked all the fat and gristle off their bones too. Uncle Bernie said he'd never seen anything like it, he just about died laughing when he saw you pack it down like that. You were really something. Christ. How much you want?

ANNIE: Just make enough for you. *(Pause.)* God my feet hurt.

JACK: You know the minute I sit down with mine you're gonna want it yourself.

ANNIE: No, the minute you sit down with yours I'm going to puke on the table, that's what I'm going to do. I hate that stuff. Pig brains.

JACK: Puke on the dress if you can help it. Christ.

ANNIE: What do you care? I paid for it, it's not your money.

JACK: I just think it's hilarious you hadda spend a whole paycheck on that when we gotta shower curtain that looks better. *(Pause.)* Who picked the color? Makes me think of bathroom sponges.

ANNIE: It's not that bad.

JACK: If you're goddamn Helen Keller.

ANNIE: 'Goddamn Helen Keller.' Nice. *(Pause.)* There are worse dresses.

JACK: I'm sure there are.

ANNIE: There are.

JACK: You get seventy-two down yet?

ANNIE: Didn't look at it.

JACK: So I'm telling you look at it. Help me out here.

ANNIE: You take your heart pills?

JACK: Sure.

ANNIE: Sure?

JACK: Yeah.

> *(Annie regards him for a moment. Jack continues bustling around the kitchen and does not look at her. She goes over to the counter by the phone and pokes through a clutter of bills and keys until she finds a plastic pill tray, the kind with each day of the week marked.)*

ANNIE: Saturday. You didn't take them.

JACK: Huh?

ANNIE: You didn't take them. You got four in here which means you didn't take them all day.

JACK: So leave them out. I'll take them now.

ANNIE: No, you can't double up or—

JACK: Christ, Annie, then I'll take the nighttime ones. I'm fine. You want maybe just a roll then? Toast? We got some bread I think—

> *(Annie shakes her head. Jack resumes his scrapple preparations. Annie takes two of the Saturday pills, pours him a glass of water from the tap, and places it all by his plate.)*

JACK: Get a coaster.

ANNIE: It's fine.

JACK: It's gonna leave a water stain.

ANNIE: *(Gets a coaster for the glass of water, sits down.)* It's a stupid table for a kitchen. Wood's supposed to go in the dining room. That's why people have Formica.

JACK: I like it here.

ANNIE: Which one am I supposed to be looking at?

JACK: Seventy-two down. And forty-four across.

ANNIE: I never get them. Why are you even asking me.

JACK: You can get them, you just don't have the patience for it. It's good for you. *(Looking in the fridge.)* How about eggs? You want eggs? Not your whipped things—

ANNIE: Whipped things.

JACK: Aw, Christ, you know what I mean, the EGGS you had earlier. The fancy ones. Not those, but an omelet, I could make you that instead.

ANNIE: You always try to make me eat eggs. I hate eggs.

JACK: You just said you had fancy eggs.

ANNIE: I did. I just don't like how you make them. They turn out scrambled no matter what you do to them.

JACK: Look, I don't give a rat's ass, I'm just saying maybe you should eat. You don't look good.

ANNIE: I don't feel good.

JACK: It shows.

ANNIE: Right.

JACK: Christ, there's always something with you. Try to relax, Anne.

ANNIE: My stomach hurts.

JACK: No, your stomach's higher up. Here. *(Indicating actual stomach placement.)*

ANNIE: You get any flutters today?

JACK: Guy walks into a doctor's office. He says, hey, Doctor, it hurts when I do this. *(Swings arm loosely from the elbow.)* Doctor says, don't do that.

ANNIE: You have pain today?

JACK: Nothing bad. So what the hell is seventy-two down, Anne? You went to college, show me all that money of mine went to some good.

ANNIE: You always finish the damn things, you don't need me. *(Pause, sighs.)* 'Mother of Apollo.'

JACK: They're making them harder lately. I used to enjoy them. Now they give me a goddamn headache.

ANNIE: I thought it was a wolf.

JACK: What?

ANNIE: The mother. Of Apollo.

JACK: I never heard of that. *(Pause.)* I thought they meant the space shuttle or something with stars and crap. *(Pause.)* The guy Rocky fought.

ANNIE: I think they're talking about, you know, the first Apollo.
(Annie continues to regard the puzzle. Jack takes a beer out of the refrigerator and stares at her.)

JACK: How could a wolf raise a human being? Are you telling me a wolf could give milk to a kid?

ANNIE: I don't know, I read it. *(Noticing his beer.)* Dad, come on. It's 2:30 in the morning.

JACK: *(Overlapping.)* What, you mean like the kid in The Jungle Book movie?

Christ, they don't show him sucking milk outta animals in that, do they? That movie was for kids. I know I woulda remembered that.

ANNIE: A female wolf could feed a human baby if she had to. It's not that different.

JACK: Aw Jesus Christ, Annie, between your dress and the wolf titties you're making me gag.

ANNIE: You asked.

(Jack sits down beside her at the table with his scrapple, his beer, a coaster, a bottle of ketchup and a bag of Wonderbread.)

JACK: Forget that one. Look at forty-four across.

ANNIE: You figure it out. I've got a headache.

JACK: *(Looking at the puzzle.)* You give me a headache. Who's Medusa?

ANNIE: The one with snakes on her head. The one you couldn't look at.

JACK: Yeah?

ANNIE: Or you'd turn to stone.

JACK: Christ. *(Pause.)* You look in a mirror lately?

ANNIE: No—

JACK: Don't. *(Laughs.)* You're turning my scrapple to stone. Tastes like dirt right now. What's all that ink under your eyes?

(Jack takes his thumb, reaches to rub the smudge under Annie's eyes. Annie stiffens, almost imperceptibly.)

ANNIE: Is it so hard to remember how to say 'mascara.'

JACK: 'Mascara.' It's ink. It's dirt. You pay what, three bucks? For dirt to rub under your eyes. Pink dirt for your cheeks. Ridiculous.

ANNIE: I never heard you complain about the dirt all over Mom's face when you used to take her out to Vitale's.

JACK: Your mother was a different story.

ANNIE: Why?

JACK: She didn't need that makeup crap, it was just icing on the cake for her.

ANNIE: I thought you were saying I don't need it either—

JACK: Oh yeah, YOU need it. You don't need to BUY it is what I'm saying. Next time you run out you let me know, I'll dig up some nice fresh dirt from the backyard for you, mix it up with a little food coloring. All set for your next wedding.

(Jack attacks his scrapple as Annie watches. "Hold Me, Thrill Me, Kiss Me" is heard on the radio. They listen in silence for a few moments, then Annie jumps up to shut it off.)

JACK: What the hell did you shut it off for? It was nice.

ANNIE: The band sucked. My ears hurt.

JACK: 'My ears hurt. My stomach hurts.' Everything hurts. So go to bed.

ANNIE: I am.

> (*They sit in silence for a few long moments. Annie inspects her pantyhose, which resemble shredded wheat.*)

ANNIE: Shit.

JACK: Huh. You dance a lot?

ANNIE: A little. I don't know why they didn't just get a DJ.

JACK: How about the happy couple? They dance?

ANNIE: I think they just felt sorry for the band. God, they were so bad, it was embarrassing. Trisha and I took our drinks into the ladies' room and camped out there for a lot of it.

JACK: I bet they look real good together. She's a pretty girl.

ANNIE: *(Sharply.)* You and Mom dance a lot at your wedding?

JACK: All night.

ANNIE: Look how swell that turned out.

JACK: Christ, I even did the polka to make her family happy. She loved it, just about wet her pants laughing on the dance floor the way I had to keep counting, one-two-HOP, one-two-HOP… My heart would probably give out if I tried that now—

ANNIE: I'm just saying, you never know if it's going to work out because everybody looks happy at their wedding, I mean who DOESN'T look happy at their own wedding—

JACK: You'd probably be the first.

ANNIE: Thanks for understanding.

JACK: I don't. End of story.

ANNIE: So pretend.

JACK: Can't say it if I don't mean it.

ANNIE: Fine. Nothing new. Forget it.

JACK: All yours. This great guy, waiting for YOU to come around, how about that? Michael could have had anybody, but somehow he's not good enough for YOU. Apes are smarter.

ANNIE: Like I'm such a FREAK of nature that nobody would stick around—

JACK: Never once did I say you were a freak.

ANNIE: So you don't say it.

JACK: I can't help it if you're not happy in your own skin.

ANNIE: Bullshit. You could help it.

JACK: I'm not in the mood.

ANNIE: *(Pause.)* Mom said she always thought I looked more like you.

JACK: Excuse me?

ANNIE: I'm just saying. How about that.

JACK: Drop it. You're giving me indigestion.

ANNIE: *(Quietly.)* She wasn't coming back.

JACK: One more word and I am going to throw you out of here on your big butt.

ANNIE: Do it.

(Jack and Annie stare at each other for a long moment before Jack resumes work on his crossword puzzle and continues eating his scrapple. Annie watches him and begins removing her long red Lee Press-On Nails with some difficulty. Jack glances at her hands and returns to his puzzle.)

ANNIE: I don't know how you eat that stuff. It looks like a hunk of cadaver.

JACK: Fancy.

ANNIE: Megan made us wear them for pictures. They're so stupid.

JACK: I meant 'cadaver.' Huh. *(Indicating her nails.)* Look better than yours, way you chew 'em to stumps. Disgusting.

ANNIE: Trisha stabbed herself in the eye with one of these during dinner. She told me she needs to find a new roommate for October because Janine's moving out. *(Pause.)* You hear what I said?

JACK: Yeah. Trisha stabbed herself in the eye.

ANNIE: It's a really cute apartment.

JACK: Uh-huh.

ANNIE: So...I might do it.

JACK: Really.

ANNIE: Thinking about it.

JACK: Where is it?

ANNIE: Sixth and Catherine.

JACK: Isn't that a lezzie neighborhood?

ANNIE: No.

JACK: Don't give me that, when I ate near there with your Uncle Bernie six months ago I saw two girls lick each other on the face.

ANNIE: *(Caught off-guard, laughs.)* What?

JACK: *(Trying not to smile.)* Christ, I get sick just thinking about it. Is Trisha—

ANNIE: No! Why would you think that?

(Jack shrugs, smirking.)

ANNIE: She isn't.

JACK: Sure.

ANNIE: *(Still laughing.)* I'm not either in case you were wondering—

JACK: Never said you were.

ANNIE: *(Venturing, gently.)* It's not far from where Mom—

JACK: I don't need to know where. Save it.

ANNIE: *(Stung.)* Fine. Thought you might want to know—

JACK: So, too bad you can't afford it.

ANNIE: I could afford it. It's not impossible—

JACK: Sure. Car payments, school loans, credit cards up the wazoo.

ANNIE: I could sell the car. I wouldn't need it down there. Take SEPTA to work.

JACK: And what the hell would I do, Annie? You stop to think of that?

ANNIE: Of course I did but there's got to be a better w—

JACK: No! Not with the goddamn doctor telling me I can't work! Christ, Annie, I'm down to fifteen hours at the bar, I only got partial coverage, we're still paying off the goddamn hospital for your mother...You tell me how I keep the house going if you run off now.

ANNIE: Maybe it's not my problem anymore—

JACK: Jesus, Annie, don't humiliate me here. I'd lose the goddamn house without your paycheck right now. Don't make me say it again. It's not forever. Just until I'm doing better. Just until I'm back up to full-time.

ANNIE: And what if you can't go back to full-time?

JACK: We deal with it then.

ANNIE: No.

JACK: *(Surprised.)* No what.

ANNIE: Just...no.

JACK: You think I want it this way? Christ.

ANNIE: Playing house. Like she's coming back.

JACK: Yeah, you tell me who wants to play house. Goddamn lezzie dollhouse with Trisha. Sure, go on, sit there and sulk. *(Jack gets up and goes to the refrigerator for another beer.)* It's the wedding that's got you like this. You're fine any other day of the week.

ANNIE: 'Fine.'

JACK: You get by. That's what I'm saying. *(Pause.)* I told you you shouldn't have gone. It was dumb. Glutton for punishment.

ANNIE: They asked me. It was the right thing—

JACK: If it was the right thing then why was it so goddamn hard for you to get up this morning? I had to bang on your door for ten minutes—

ANNIE: I know you don't get it okay—

JACK: I don't know how you even looked at your own face this morning, that's the God's honest truth. *(Pause.)* So how did it feel, anyway. Watching him marry somebody else. I'll admit it, I'm dying to hear you say it.

ANNIE: There's nothing to say anymore, we're all friends, it's fine—

JACK: Aw yeah, friends, the best. HAH. Christ, come on, you think Megan asked you to be one of her bridesmaids because she wanted to share all her happy feelings with you? Is that what you told yourself?

ANNIE: No—

JACK: Megan wanted you there to say look what you gave up, and he wanted you there to show you he DID find better, and good for both of them, I say. Nice they found each other.

ANNIE: Like you've never been in a hard place—

JACK: I have been in Michael's place, and that is a VERY different place to be from wherever the hell you are.

ANNIE: All I'm asking is that you show a little compassion, I'm your daughter for God's sake—

JACK: You want me to feel sorry for you? You're the one telling me how easy it is to be their buddy, their good buddy Annie. *(Pause.)* So how did he look?

ANNIE: You kill me. You're hilarious, you know that?

JACK: I bet he looked very handsome. He is a very good-looking guy, you can't tell me you don't still see it—

ANNIE: What the hell, I didn't say I don't see it, of course I see it, I never said there was anything wrong with him that way, we have been through this so many times, I swear to God. It's like you were sleeping with him—

JACK: I don't have to be a faggot to see he was as good as it's ever going to get for you. I'm sorry. I'm your father and nobody else has the balls to tell you the truth here—

ANNIE: Listen to yourself! I tell you it wasn't right for me and you go on for years like I gave away the…the Kingdom of God or—

JACK: No, YOU gave away Showcase Number One…and there's nothing behind Showcase Number Two. I hate to break it to you, Annie, but you get the Turtle Wax and the goddamn vacuum and that's just the way it is—congratulations, Annie.

ANNIE: You should write for TV.

JACK: I'm a funny guy.

ANNIE: So I got you instead of the convertible.

JACK: You got Trisha. She's your consolation prize.

ANNIE: I know you don't get it, but people…people find their soulmate at the drugstore, crash into them in line someplace, the pet store, it happens. He's out there and I'm going to find him—

JACK: Oh yeah, he's out there, with the friggin UFOs. *(Muttering.)* Goddamn Oprah Winfrey.

ANNIE: It wasn't Michael! Everybody thought I was so lucky but he didn't know me, not how I wanted—

JACK: How did you want it?

ANNIE: *(Searching for the words.)* I—I wanted him to—

JACK: To what?

ANNIE: I just…I'll know. I know I'll know. You have to believe me—

JACK: Oh for Christ's sake.

ANNIE: It wasn't Michael—and you weren't Mom's.

JACK: You don't know a goddamn thing about what it takes to—

ANNIE: Mom found him. Her soulmate.

JACK: Soulmate. Christ. Your mother was so full of morphine before she died she didn't know what the hell she was saying. That guy was nothing to her—

ANNIE: You're pathetic, you're still hanging on to this stupid idea that somehow she would have come back to you! You think you loved her that that was LOVE—

JACK: I didn't think it, I KNEW IT and SHE knew it—

ANNIE: No! You didn't love her like she needed!

JACK: What the hell do you know about it—

ANNIE: You act like I wasn't there! Your only kid, I was there all the time, I saw how you were—

JACK: I was GOOD to her I treated her to treats—

ANNIE: You left her alone! You made her feel stupid like she wasn't smart enough! *(Pause.)* I saw you hit her.

JACK: NO!

ANNIE: I saw you hit her here in the kitchen. You hit her so hard she went down on her knees.

JACK: BULLSHIT!

ANNIE: How can you look me in the face and tell me I didn't see it?

JACK: I hit her ONCE in our whole life together! ONCE!

ANNIE: I SAW you hit her once. Did you hit her more?

JACK: ONCE!

ANNIE: Really?

JACK: ONE TIME! Don't you dare question me!

ANNIE: *(Quietly.)* So tell me, who should I ask?

JACK: You smell. What, you forget to wear deodorant today? Bad move, Annie, I'm sure they were already laughing their asses off that you fell for their big bridesmaid joke—

(Annie stares at him, then wheels around and goes to the stove. She grabs the kettle and begins filling it with water.)

ANNIE: You want some tea? I'm going to make tea.

JACK: I don't drink tea. I'm going to bed.

ANNIE: Mom and I had tea every Saturday afternoon. After she moved into her own place.

JACK: So? What the hell does goddamn tea mean?

ANNIE: She took a ceramics class. She made teacups. One with her name and one with my name and I'm saying we had tea in them. In her apartment.

JACK: So what? You think you're gonna make me cry over teacups? Get over yourself.

ANNIE: She loved that apartment, it was over an Italian bakery. God it smelled good—

JACK: Maybe you should live over a bakery. Look at you, sweating like a pig—

ANNIE: Even when she stopped eating at least she could smell the bread. Sometimes, when he'd visit, he'd bring her a fresh loaf from the bakery. She'd just bury her face in it. She said she liked the smell so much, it made her forget she couldn't eat it...and he'd just smile at her—

JACK: She was fooling herself! She was fooling you! She was so lonely I bet she couldn't see straight—

ANNIE: Lonely? Is that what you think? He was with her all the time, she turned into a...a flower with him She was huge, the tumor was eating all the weight off her bones and I swear to God she was still getting bigger somehow. She filled up every room when she was with him! She was beautiful!

JACK: She was beautiful with me!

ANNIE: We don't even have pictures of her the last few years she was here with us! It kills me, she'd take pictures of you and me at Christmas or my graduation and we didn't even THINK to take any with her—

JACK: We've got plenty of pictures, I'll get em out if you don't believe me

ANNIE: I'm telling you he has more pictures of her from their one year together than you have from almost a life with her. What do you think of that?

JACK: You don't know what the hell you're talking about, I gave your mother EVERYTHING she wanted! I loved her! *(Jack gets up and begins pounding on different appliances, the cherry-wood table.)* THIS! And THIS! This table from the Spiegel's catalog for our fifteenth anniversary, because she cried when she saw it! Because she knew we didn't have the money! You should have seen the way she ran to it when it got delivered. She petted this table for three hours like she was petting a goddamn cat!

ANNIE: That doesn't take it away—

JACK: YES! It does! She forgot about that one mistake and so did I! And THAT is love, Annie, that's what it's about, and that's the kind of thing that makes you come back, she was coming back to me.

ANNIE: If it meant so much, why'd she leave it here when she left you?

JACK: As an anchor! She was still anchored to me and I knew it. You're anchored to Michael even if you don't know it, someday you're gonna FEEL that pull, and you are gonna hurt like hell—

ANNIE: Would you shut up about him if I told you he hit me?

JACK: He didn't!

ANNIE: What if he did? Would it matter?

JACK: What are you trying to do, did he or didn't he?

ANNIE: One time.

JACK: No!

ANNIE: *(Overlapping.)* No, he didn't! But he raised his hand to me once. And I shut my eyes and went down on my knees anyway. When I look he's standing on the other side of his mom's kitchen holding his fist inside the freezer door. I don't know what the hell he thought that was going to do, but I didn't care anyway, that was it—

JACK: Don't be like that, Annie! A man raises a hand to you in a fit of anger, it happens! It's human nature! I'm not saying it's right, but I'm saying it happens!

ANNIE: It doesn't just HAPPEN! There's something so wrong if it just HAP-PENS! Who's to say he wouldn't have hit me the next time and knocked me on my ass? I didn't know, maybe that's what Mom did with you— she told herself you wouldn't hit her again, that it wouldn't happen again—

JACK: And it didn't! It never happened again! You count your goddamn blessings that you've got anybody at all—

ANNIE: I don't see you counting any blessings that you've still got me! Your ugly duckling, always a bridesmaid, right?

JACK: *(Ignoring her.)* You...you BITE your tongue once in awhile and you get through. That's how you get through the hard times—

ANNIE: Mom bit her tongue for twenty-nine years. I don't remember you having to bite too hard—

JACK: You have this idea in your head, but you don't know your father, Annie.

I don't know who you think you know but it's not me. *(Pause.)* You go, fine, you move in with Trisha, I don't give a damn where you go—

ANNIE: I think she would have chewed it off. If she had stayed with you.

JACK: What?

ANNIE: She could have bitten her tongue straight through and fried it up with your scrapple and you wouldn't have noticed—

JACK: You're drunk. Aren't you. That's what I'm smelling. Real becoming, Annie. Jesus, you probably made an ass of yourself at the wedding, bet his parents really enjoyed that—

ANNIE: Blood instead of ketchup. Her blood instead of your ketchup, and her little pink tongue all curled up on the side of your plate—

JACK: *(Starting to scrape the scrapple into the sink.)* I'm getting rid of this. It's going in the garbage with the rest of the crap coming out of your mouth tonight—

ANNIE: Did you hear what I said?

JACK: No. Go to bed. You're a goddamn mess and now you're not making any sense. I've never seen you like this. I didn't realize you were drunk—

ANNIE: I'm not, don't walk away! Watch me eat it, watch me eat your goddamn scrapple—

(Annie grabs the plate of now-cold scrapple from him and begins shoving chunks of it in her mouth furiously.)

JACK: What the hell Annie—

ANNIE: Look at me go look at me watch me pack it down—

JACK: Sit up and knock it off. You're drunk.

ANNIE: Aw, come on, you love to watch me eat, look at me go… *(Grabs bread, mops plate with it, squirts ketchup on it.)* …I'm going to bite off my tongue for you—and you won't have to hear it anymore—

JACK: Christ Annie I mean it—

ANNIE: NO, you watch this, I'm eating this for you and you are going to watch me, okay? *(Shoves scrapple into her mouth and chews violently.)* LOOK DAD NO HANDS! THIS ONE'S FOR YOU—

JACK: You're disgusting. Knock it off and spit it out. Spit it out. SPIT IT OUT.

(Annie shakes her head and reaches for more bread. Jack knocks the bread on the floor and shakes her hard. She begins coughing.)

JACK: *(Grabbing her.)* Jesus Christ! Spit it out, for Christ's sake, spit it out on the floor! I'll clean it up, okay, just get it out—

ANNIE: *(Still coughing.)* You shouldn't…should NOT have stopped me. Why did you stop me?

JACK: What the hell are you saying? You're gonna give me another heart attack, I swear to God, Annie, my heart is pounding like a—

ANNIE: You don't feel it as much with the bread. I could have bitten straight through, I wouldn't have felt it. Then it would be quiet around here quiet just how you like it—

JACK: You've got real problems Annie real problems—

ANNIE: I am so good and you don't see it! Nobody sees! Michael had no idea, he couldn't see two inches into me and I'm supposed to be grateful? I don't want somebody who could ever raise a hand to me but it's more than that...I want somebody who's gonna help me find the words... somebody who's gonna think I'm beautiful! And brave! Walking away from him wasn't stupid, it was brave! I am so much bigger than you know but somebody has to help me get it all out... (*Laughing, dissolving.*) ...It's never gonna come out now, is it? If you're goddamn Helen Keller you get a goddamn Miracle Worker. I need a Miracle Worker and all I've got left is you. So what do you say, Dad? Wanna be my Miracle Worker? Say you will. Because I need one god I need one so bad—

(*She laughs hysterically. The laughter eventually subsides into sobs. Jack stares at her, fists clenched. After a few moments of watching her cry, he looks around the kitchen. He grabs a roll of paper towels, hesitates, then rips off a few and nudges them very gently at her arm.*)

JACK: Annie. Annie. Come on, here, clean up your face. Annie. (*Pause.*) Honey? (*Blackout.*)

END OF PLAY

Prelude to a Crisis

BY ARI ROTH

THE AUTHOR

Ari Roth received the 1990 Clifford Davie Award for his play *Oh, The Innocents* which premiered at GeVa Theater, directed by Joe Mantello. That same year, he was commissioned by Arena Stage to adapt *Born Guilty*, Peter Sichrovsky's book of interviews with children of Nazis, where the play was directed by Founding Producer Zelda Fichandler and nominated for the Helen Hayes Award for Best New Play. *Born Guilty* was produced Off-Broadway at the American Jewish Theater in a widely acclaimed extended run and has received over a dozen subsequent productions across the country. His play *Goodnight Irene* was commissioned by Manhattan Theater Club with a grant from the National Foundation for Jewish Culture and has been produced at Performance Network in Ann Arbor, Michigan, directed by Gilbert McCauley, and at Theater J in Washington, DC where Roth currently serves as Artistic Director.

For Theater J, he has produced David Mamet's *The Old Neighborhood*, Neena Beber's *Tomorrowland*, Motti Lerner's *Exile In Jerusalem* and Clifford Odets' *Waiting For Lefty* for which he contributed an original companion piece, *Still Waiting*. He recently received a National Endowment For The Arts Workshop Grant for *Remaking A Melting Pot*, nominated by Northlight Theater. Other recent plays include *Life In Refusal* (Performance Network) and *Love And Yearning In The Not For Profits* which appeared at the HB Playwrights Foundation Museum Play Festival.

Roth is a two-time winner of the Helen Eisner Award and the Avery Hopwood Award for Drama from the University of Michigan where he was a student and then served on the faculty in the English Department for nine years. More recently he has taught at Brandeis University and in New York University's Dramatic Writing Program.

ORIGINAL PRODUCTION

Prelude To A Crisis was first presented in 1997 at the HB Playwrights Foundation Motel Play Festival, with Peter Birkenhead and Elizabeth Bunch, directed by Amy Wright. It was produced at the Ensemble Studio Theatre's Marathon '98, the 21st Annual Festival of One-Act Plays (Curt Dempster, Artistic Director; Jamie Richards, Executive Producer) in New York City, June, 1998. It was directed by Mark Nelson with the following cast:

THE TEACHER . . . . Greg Germann
THE STUDENT. . . . . Melinda Page Hamilton

CHARACTERS
THE TEACHER
NICKI
DEBBIE

SETTING
A room in a faculty lodge at a major state university in the Midwest.

TIME
Present.

There is a phone by a bed, a bottle of wine and a small box in a paper bag. Two chairs and a table. A man waits for the phone, writes, stops, crumples; then in a burst.

TEACHER: I'm gonna say something and it's gonna smack of defensiveness but that's what I am these days—I am a wall of it. I am the Berlin Wall of Confidence. And so what if it's unappealing? I'd pre*fer* me as confident. I'd prefer me employed. Which I may not be. Not up to me. What's up to me is my conscience and I've decided to Come Out about it so here goes...

I forgot what I was gonna say. I-was-gonna-*say*-something; it-was-gonna-smack-of-defensiveness-but-that's-what-I-*am*; I am a *wall*...I honestly hate this device. I'm forever telling my students how much I hate this kind of device! Man alone, in a room, wondering *aloud* whether some pixie of an honors student is ever gonna show—Okay, there...I gave a very promising honors student my room number about three hours ago. And I'm up for re-appointment. I'm gonna start over.
(Clears throat. A different tack; cheerful.)

I'm assuming this isn't done. I've certainly never done this! I've only *imagined* giving an honors student my room number, and now *acting* upon it, I take it as a sign of Growth; and Strength; and Maturity; or Stupidity; could be that.

Actually, it's not even the room number; it's the extension, but they're the same and she can figure it out—"Either call or come by." That's how we left it. Apparently, my hotel is on the way back to the *sorority*, so...Um, she's not really an honor's student. I just made that up to look better; or feel better, which is truly insane, given how I anticipate feeling at the end of this interlude. Not that I have any *experience* with these kinds of interludes. Or more accurately, I barely... "Either call or come by." That's how we left it. Big Reading tomorrow. End-of-Term Presentations. That's why I'm staying over—That, and a quickie with the Chair—Meeting—About next year. Haven't heard, but not to worry. "All gonna sail though." That's what my wife says, but I mean, what does *she* really know? Which is an interesting question; or *the* interesting question, given what I'm doing here; that I've actually bought a bottle of *Fetzer Merlot*—I don't even drink Merlot! But maybe she *does* know; my wife; about the job; and I'll keep it; which is needed. Extremely needed. Given our situation—A gig like this is a gift! You wanna hold onto it. Not fuck it up! Not invite some pixie-of an-honors-student-who's-not-even-an-honors-student up for drinks or anything boneheaded, which I didn't. *Her* suggestion. I think that's important to establish; that she was nervous about her climax. That's what she said, half-smiling, in that flirty, office-hour banter we sometimes get into.

STUDENT: *(Appearing, in the bathroom doorway.)* I guess I'm just nervous!

TEACHER: See?

STUDENT: About my climax.

TEACHER: It's not really your climax; it's your crisis; that's what I told her.

STUDENT: And the difference...?

TEACHER: And of course she *knows* the difference. She isn't aware she's in one. Or that her character; that she's passing through one. Tricky thing, the Crisis; if you're in one. Some speak of it as a Turning Point. Others, mistakenly, still think of it as "The Break-Down." Text-book phrasing I prefer: "The point where the dominant question no longer needs to be articulated, it's that obvious," and *Debbie's* dominant—

STUDENT: "Should I or should I not leave the bathroom and get married to that dentist?"

TEACHER: And underlying that...

STUDENT: "Did Mommy really kill herself just 'cause Daddy had one stupid, bone headed affair?"

(She looks at him. Beat. He clears throat.)

TEACHER: ...Y'know something? This device isn't any better. Either come in or leave—Okay, thanks.

STUDENT: ...*You're in a mood.*

TEACHER: This isn't "mood." You're not even here yet; have a seat. I tried looking down her sweater today. Can I say that? I'm saying it. Debbie was leaning over to open her computer—Um, I probably shouldn't be using her name; I should probably change it to Jenny; or Nikki. Nikki looks up, as if to say—

NIKKI: Whattayou looking at?

TEACHER: Nothing. Because I wasn't! I couldn't see anything. Except for the freckles. I'd never noticed freckles before and her chest was quite full of them. Quite lovely too; her sternum. I didn't notice the breasts. Which were pert. But there was something sun-burst about her face, like she had just come in from the cold and her cheeks had found the experience exhilarating and were now ANNOUNCING it out loud! Her lip gloss was glistening, brown like butterscotch. And I appreciated her blue jeans. I've actually *only* seen her in blue jeans, and I appreciate knowing that this is a rich kid—Buffalo money—and you can tell by her teeth;

by her rings, which are several, with diamonds more numerous than anything I could dream of giving, that this girl was at least making the at*tempt* of appearing to have virtually no wardrobe, and I respect that in an undergraduate!

NIKKI: *(Impatient, prodding.)* So I'm *bending over?* You're smelling my lip gloss and looking at my freckles but *not* my breasts…?

TEACHER: So she's "unvelcro-ing" the flap to her computer case when she says—

NIKKI: *(She hands him pages.)* Here. Tell me what you think.

TEACHER: I begin to read. She begins to fidget. And slouch. In her chair. She could be *twelve.* Asks if I have anything she could read while she's waiting.

NIKKI: Well?

TEACHER: Starts to look on my desk. Starts to look *in* my desk.

NIKKI: What's this?

TEACHER: What are you doing?

NIKKI: I asked you first.

TEACHER: I'm dumping that.

NIKKI: Can I read it?

TEACHER: No.

NIKKI: Why not?

TEACHER: Cause you're *in it.*

NIKKI: Really?…So why's it called, "The Professor And The Whore?"

TEACHER: I can't tell you that.

NIKKI: That is such a *tease.*

TEACHER: Which hits home, because in high-school, I think I was the only *non-female* ever to be called "tease," although a more accurate description probably would've been, "Coward-with-aggression-and-over-supplicant-smile." Better stick with tease. And she's right. If I wanna tell her, I should tell, but don't play "peek-a-boo" and then—

NIKKI: *(Retrieving her pages.)* I don't have time for old stuff. I need to show you something new.

TEACHER: She starts booting up her lap-top. We both know what this means.

NIKKI: It means I haven't had time to "Print" but I'd still like you to look.

TEACHER: And by look, she means over her shoulder, just like that day after class—

NIKKI: Just press the cursor when you need to.

TEACHER: *"And so you're pressing her cursor; plunging the arrow down-down, and she's letting you, peruse her, with your finger, and she's enjoying it; you can tell; by her sternum…* " And this is the part you wanna show her; because she inspired it; that day after class—But you don't dare. Besides, you're dumping it—That's what you do: You cut; you gut; you flush. *Of course, first you've spilled!* And it's at this point, she says something that can only be described as generous and potentially quite liberating.

NIKKI: If I tell you a secret, will you tell me one of yours?

TEACHER: …Deal.

NIKKI: I can never show this play to my family.

TEACHER: Y'mean, because of…because…your mother? Because she…

NIKKI: Killed herself?

TEACHER: Uh-huh.

NIKKI: My mother never *killed* herself!

TEACHER: She didn't?

NIKKI: My father's never had an affair!

TEACHER: Are you sure?

NIKKI: Of course, I'm sure! What do you mean, am I sure? I mean, I *think* I'm—

TEACHER: Good. That's…Good inventing.

NIKKI: But I'm not! That's why I can't show this! Cause y'know how the sister? The older sister? The maid-of-honor who's got the boyfriend who's also her very married boss, only the parents don't know, they think he's some kinda Jewish Prince who just shows up for holidays and the only person who knows the truth is the younger sister in the bathroom, just like me in real life?

TEACHER: *(Not following.)* …Uh-huh?

NIKKI: I mean, isn't that, like, a violation? Like, she's confided some things that could get her *fired,* and now I'm *telling* you, and not *just* you, but the class, and not just the class, but the whole—

TEACHER: And I guess I find this fascinating because I'm seeing, I've created a protégé, and that we now share a legacy of spilling secrets to the world that we wouldn't dare tell our families! As she goes on about some un*believably* torrid affair—

NIKKI: And so this traveling prince is always flying off on business and he'll fly Heather out to Cleveland, or Dallas, just for the night, and they'll fuck 'till the dawn—

TEACHER: And I'm thinking, "*Why* is she telling me this?"

NIKKI: Go through an entire box of condoms in one night—

TEACHER: And I'm thinking, "I don't get through an entire box of condoms in one *year!* I got trouble just *buying* the things!" Maybe *that's why* she's telling me!

NIKKI: And then the Me-Character-Behind-The-Door slumps to the floor and goes, "There is so much more to life than I've experienced, and I should probably *do* something about that... don'tchya think?"

TEACHER: ...And she closed up her lap top.

NIKKI: But we still haven't finished, right? I mean, that's just her crisis. We still haven't gotten to the climax.

TEACHER: Right.

NIKKI: And I wanna get to one. Before you leave.

TEACHER: And she looked at me like she knew something.

NIKKI: Well? Any ideas?

TEACHER: "Write a speech," I told her; a speech for your Me-Character. Y'know, your Me-Behind-The-Door? Have her open it. Come out. Make a move.

NIKKI: But where? Speech about what?

TEACHER: Whatever's unexamined. Like her parents' marriage; quite potentially her own?

NIKKI: And can I show you what I come up with before the reading?

TEACHER: Sure.

NIKKI: Like maybe later?

TEACHER: Sure.

NIKKI: Tonight?

TEACHER: And she asked if I had a phone and so I gave her the extension, and she said...

NIKKI: *(Goes to door, then stops.)* ...Do *all* fathers have affairs? I mean, where the kids know. Or just the wives? Or *do* the wives? Find out. Would yours? Not that you would; I mean, *everyone knows*—they wouldn't come to Office Hours if they thought you did—but *if* you did...Would you?

TEACHER: Would I...?

NIKKI: Tell?

TEACHER: I think it would have to come out.

NIKKI: It would?

TEACHER: Eventually. I think so. One way or another.

NIKKI: That is *so* admirable!

TEACHER: It is?

NIKKI: See ya! *(She leaves.)*

TEACHER: And she was gone!

(Lights shift. Phone rings. With trepidation, he goes to the bed, sits, and answers.)

TEACHER: *(On phone.)* Hello. Hi. Nope. So you're...? Wow. Great! Well, I can

come down if you just wanna…Uh-huh? Or you could just as easily…
Sure, come up, if…"What floor?" Well, let's…"Just like the extension!"
Yup. "That's what the *three's* for!" "*See* ya." *(Hangs up.)* Shit.
(Straightens up. A knock at the door.)

STUDENT: *(Off.)* It's me!

TEACHER: Shit! I mean, *coming!*

STUDENT: Hello? *(She enters, wearing a sweater.)*

TEACHER: Nikki.

STUDENT: Who?

TEACHER: Nothing. Hi.

STUDENT: Hi.

TEACHER: Hi.

STUDENT: Who's the wine for?

TEACHER: Wine? Oh, no one. It's just, y'know; wine. It's there. Merlot.

STUDENT: I don't drink Merlot.

TEACHER: Neither do I.

STUDENT: So why'd you buy it?

TEACHER: Just in case.

STUDENT: In *case?*

TEACHER: I change my mind. 'Bout what I do—I mean, *drink.* If I get thirsty?

STUDENT: Cool. So is that a Gobstopper in there?

TEACHER: Where?

STUDENT: The box? In the bag? 'Cause you always bring vanilla yogurt and a
box of Gobstoppers to class, which is, like, total contradiction, but that's
the point, right? That you're making? About Drama?

TEACHER: Point?

STUDENT: That "a character's breadth is measured by the width of his con-
tradictions."

TEACHER: Which would make me a very Dramatic Eater.

STUDENT: Or a hypocrite. I'm taking one.

TEACHER: No! I mean, I'd pre*fer*—I mean, you could, if they *were,* but they're
not so—

STUDENT: So what are they?

TEACHER: …Cigarettes.

STUDENT: I thought you don't smoke.

TEACHER: I don't.

STUDENT: But "just in *case?*"

TEACHER: Uh-huh!? *(He stuffs the bag in a pocket.)*

STUDENT: I like that! That is a great way of going through life!

TEACHER: What? Y'mean, defensive?

STUDENT: Prepared. For the unexpected. Oh, and I've already had a pack. I was nervous. Before. About coming over. Now I'm not.

TEACHER: Good.

STUDENT: Now I'm mostly intrigued.

TEACHER: So! You wanna show me what you been working on?

STUDENT: Y'know, I was mad at you.

TEACHER: You were?

STUDENT: Before? In the library? I mean, I'm doing the assignment, and all of a sudden I go, *"Why* am I doing this assignment? Are *you* doing this assignment? Do teachers ever *do* the assignments they assign?"

TEACHER: So it made you...?

STUDENT: "Uncomfortable?" Yes, I'd say—

TEACHER: Because sometimes that can be, y'know, a *good* thing.

STUDENT: Oh, it can be a *great* thing! I think *everyone* should throw out an entire semester's work the night before Finals.

TEACHER: Well, no, I know the timing—

STUDENT: I think *everyone* should have their Me-Characters examine their parents' marriage or *quite potentially their own* and then *do something about it!*

TEACHER: So does she?

STUDENT: Did you?

TEACHER: Did I?

STUDENT: Do the assignment?

TEACHER: I have.

STUDENT: You've examined a marriage.

TEACHER: Uh-huh.

STUDENT: Quite potentially your own?

TEACHER: I...

STUDENT: And what have you done about it?

TEACHER: I've...stayed married.

STUDENT: Uh-huh.

TEACHER: What?

STUDENT: Nothing. Just you keep asking all these questions about my father.

TEACHER: I thought you were the one asking *me.* Specifically, "Do all fathers have affairs?"

STUDENT: I was asking in general.

TEACHER: It didn't *seem* all that general—

STUDENT: Well, maybe that's *your* problem.

TEACHER: Maybe.

STUDENT: So do they?

TEACHER: Does yours? In the piece.

STUDENT: Well, there was this baby-sitter, in Spain. Who used to wash her hair in the moonlight, and maybe his too, but why? Why would a man—this happily married father—risk everything just to watch some girl come home from the discos and take off all her clothes, and did he really follow her down one night to the patio, or is that not believable? See, that's when I stopped, because how would I know? If it's real? If I've never lived it? See what I mean?

TEACHER: Why don't I just read it?

STUDENT: Because it isn't finished! I mean, there's still a ton of questions, like, if he goes back—or *why* would he go back—to his wife—if it's so romantic under the moon? See, I'd say in stirring things up, I've lost what I had, and what I thought was my crisis, that's just prelude to a crisis, and all the Spain stuff raises *new* questions, besides getting married—Forget the getting married. I CUT the whole getting married!

TEACHER: You cut the whole getting…?

STUDENT: Now it's, should she go overseas for the year, or stay put and see if it changes; the situation; *his* situation; because it's an *unclear* situation.

TEACHER: What situation are we talking about?

STUDENT: With the man she's in love with.

TEACHER: You mean, the dentist?

STUDENT: Only he's not a dentist anymore, I changed that too.

TEACHER: So what is he now?

STUDENT: A teacher.

TEACHER: I see…

STUDENT: Her teacher.

TEACHER: …Isn't he supposed to be married?

STUDENT: So?

TEACHER: Right. "So." So, what's the effect of this affair? On your character? Of her father's. With the baby-sitter. If he had one.

STUDENT: It frees her.

TEACHER: Really? Wow! So what does she decide? Your Character?

STUDENT: Well, again. That depends. On him. Cause she isn't sure they even *see* each other again.

TEACHER: Yes, you keep saying.

STUDENT: Well, it's true! And whether she should be controlled by the fact

that he's her teacher; or if he's not, then should she wait for him? Or he
   for her? See what I mean?

TEACHER: What do you mean "if he's not?"

STUDENT: If he stops teaching.

TEACHER: But why would he do that? Doesn't he need to? Isn't teaching, like,
   a really important gig for him?

STUDENT: I guess. He's sort of under-developed that way. I was worried about
   that. And that it'd be hurtful. You know, to my Mom? Or my Dad? But
   I guess that doesn't matter, right? I mean, I got that from you. Cause you
   always say "Be brutally honest" and you are.

TEACHER: I am?

STUDENT: Sure. In your work! As a teacher! I mean, you'll say something in
   the course of a conversation, you'll drop some bomb that'll totally *blow
   a hole in a person's life*, then fly off; unaware; you're not around for the
   tidal wave; you're in Manhattan, making deals, living this totally high-
   rise life—

TEACHER: W-what did I say?

STUDENT: See? You don't even remember!

TEACHER: Tell me.

STUDENT: That time? In your office, when I still engaged but didn't know
   what to major in, and you said it didn't matter; that my only job was to
   become a Woman of Substance—

TEACHER: I remember that…

STUDENT: The implication being, I had *no* substance. Or if I did, I wasn't a
   woman; I was a *waif* of substance; a speck of substance; a sliver of nothing but nail polish and privilege dressed in tennis whites, and who wants
   that? Who wants what I am? I have to *change* what I am, because I am
   from suburban Buffalo and THERE ARE NO WOMEN OF SUB-
   STANCE FROM SUBURBAN BUFFALO!

TEACHER: Nikki, I didn't mean—

STUDENT: And then I started thinking about that picture; on your desk; of
   your wife.

TEACHER: Nikki—

STUDENT: Y'know, her lips are about twice the size that mine are?

TEACHER: Nikki, really—

STUDENT: That's a sign of fertility in African cultures. Is that what you meant
   when you said Woman of Substance? That I should become like your—?

TEACHER: I think you are a terrific…

STUDENT: You think I'm a *bauble,* is what you think.

TEACHER: I think you are a very impressive, young woman of—

STUDENT: Emphasis on "young."

TEACHER: Well, you are. And that's okay. Look, I didn't mean to hurt your feelings.

STUDENT: Yes, you did! You *knew* what you were saying when you said it, and that's the point: About honesty; even when it's being brutal; that it can also be kind. And liberating. You taught me that. You are the first person to have any expectations for me that weren't all about himself, and so what if that hurts? I can stand it. I am not some orchid. I can grow stalk. I can live outside the hot house.

TEACHER: Well, that sounds...good. *You* sound good.

STUDENT: I do?

TEACHER: Yeah.

STUDENT: So why do you keep calling me Nikki?

TEACHER: ...What do you mean?

STUDENT: I'm Debbie.

TEACHER: ...I know that.

DEBBIE: Do you?

TEACHER: Sure! Who's Nikki?

DEBBIE: I don't know!

TEACHER: Me neither!

DEBBIE: Cause I don't want you to get me confused with some character.

TEACHER: I agree.

DEBBIE: And I don't think it's healthy to hide behind one either. And I have been. And that's why I don't finish things.

TEACHER: 'Cause you're hiding.

DEBBIE: Haven't *you* been? *(Beat.)* You said you had a secret. That you'd tell me. Today? In your office? I think I know what it is.

TEACHER: You do?

DEBBIE: Those aren't cigarettes in that box; in the bag; in your pocket?

TEACHER: No.

DEBBIE: But you *did* buy them. Today? At a drug store.

TEACHER: Uh-huh.

DEBBIE: Because I noticed; the bag. "Campus Apothecary."

TEACHER: Good eyes.

DEBBIE: You think? So does it have to do with my sister? What you bought. And the story about and the Traveling Prince and what they *did*...

TEACHER: It's not what you're thinking.

DEBBIE: Can I *see* what you were thinking?

TEACHER: I'd rather you not.

DEBBIE: I'd rather. *(She slowly reaches into his pocket. Takes out the bag. Pulls out the box.)* "Tums...?" *(Beat.)* ...That's not what I was thinking.

TEACHER: I know.

DEBBIE: Why would anyone be embarrassed about "Tums?"

TEACHER: Because that's not what they were going to *buy*. And I don't drink Merlot either.

DEBBIE: But you bought it...

TEACHER: *"Just in case...?"*

DEBBIE: You be*come* a Merlot drinker?

TEACHER: Uh-huh.

DEBBIE: So do you wanna kiss me, Stuart?...Is that the secret you've been waiting to tell me?

TEACHER: Tell me what happens to the couple. In the story. How's it end?

DEBBIE: I'm not sure.

TEACHER: Well, how should it? How do you want it to?

DEBBIE: Well. After she comes out from behind the door; after she opens it, makes the move, she says to her teacher, "Let's do it." And they do it. And it's the *best* he's ever had, and she the same, because they understand each other; and they need each other. They get together and stay together and *get* married, and then it can end, right? Because the question's finally been answered. What's been running through the story from the start.

TEACHER: Right.

DEBBIE: Great.

TEACHER: Great.

DEBBIE: Well...?

TEACHER: Guess ya better go type it up...

DEBBIE: Really?

TEACHER: Yeah. Good story. Good end.

DEBBIE: Too bad I don't have my *lap-top*.

TEACHER: Right.

DEBBIE: *(Bending down for her bag.)* You were looking down my sweater this afternoon, weren't you? I mean, I think I could tell.

TEACHER: You...

DEBBIE: I was bending over to open my computer case. You were staring at my sternum but not my breasts—You were interested in something else; and I wondered what that was. See, I'm trying to become more aware; of the effect that I have; of the space I take up; in a room. Because that seems to me a good working definition for what a person of substance really is.

TEACHER: That sounds…

DEBBIE: Someone who takes up space. In someone's mind. A person who registers. *That's* how I think of you as being. So why pretend that you're not?

TEACHER: What do you mean?

DEBBIE: You looked down my sweater. So say it.

TEACHER: I looked…down your sweater.

DEBBIE: Why are you afraid with me? You're almost eighteen years *older* than me!

TEACHER: That's sorta the [point]…

DEBBIE: *I'm* the one who's never had a real affair. I mean, you have, haven't you? So say it! Who with?

TEACHER: Debbie.

DEBBIE: Another student?

TEACHER: No.

DEBBIE: Or a stranger? Because I saw that title. On your desk. About the Professor and the Whore—

TEACHER: That was a story.

DEBBIE: Where'd it come from?…Why'd you dump it?…Why do you stop yourself?

TEACHER: I don't always…

DEBBIE: You mostly.

TEACHER: I barely.

DEBBIE: So don't live barely anymore.

(They've moved to each other. He grabs her. A kiss. He stops. Moves to the bed. She follows, as they undress and embrace.)

DEBBIE: I mean, it's not like you're *around* next semester, so who has to know?

TEACHER: *(Continuing to kiss.)* Whaddayamean?

DEBBIE: Nothing. Just, I didn't see your name; in the course guide; so I guess you wanted to be more free, huh?

TEACHER: *(Barely listening, still kissing.)* Huh? Oh. Yeah. Right.

DEBBIE: Or was it just the commuting getting stressful? Cause it does, right?

TEACHER: Huh?

DEBBIE: So that was the secret, wasn't it? That you didn't want to tell me? That you're *leaving!*

TEACHER: Leaving?

DEBBIE: So you must've found something really *great,* huh?

TEACHER: I didn't *know* I was leaving.

DEBBIE: What do you mean?

TEACHER: I'm not in the course guide!?

DEBBIE: Didn't anybody...?

TEACHER: Who's in the course guide?

DEBBIE: Professor Haas.

TEACHER: Oh my God!

DEBBIE: Oh my God.

TEACHER: I have a meeting with the Chair; in the morning. We've been missing each other.

DEBBIE: You're just finding out *now?*

TEACHER: I'm gonna have to tell my wife.

DEBBIE: I should go.

TEACHER: Oh my God.

DEBBIE: Do you want me to? Because we could work on my scene. Or, I dunno, talk?

(No response.)

DEBBIE: So who *is* this Professor Haas anyway? Because, he couldn't be as good as you, right? I think I'll take it. Just to prove that I can do this. You know? Without a crush? Or should I go overseas?

TEACHER: Huh? Oh, sure. Whatever. Definitely. Both.

DEBBIE: Right... *(A beat of disappointment.)* Think I'm gonna change my ending. They don't get married.

TEACHER: That sounds...

DEBBIE: She goes to Spain for the year. He goes home to his wife. It doesn't end happy. But at least it's real. They have taken up space. Nothing barely about 'em.

(She exits. He is alone.)

TEACHER: Think I'm gonna have that bottle of Merlot now.

(Slow fade.)

END OF PLAY

The Trio

BY SHEL SILVERSTEIN

THE AUTHOR

Shel Silverstein was last represented on the New York stage with his play *The Devil and Billy Markham,* which played a double bill with David Mamet's *Bobby Gould In Hell,* collectively titled *Oh Hell,* at the Mitzi Newhouse Theatre at Lincoln Center. With Mr. Mamet, he co-wrote the screenplay, *Things Change* for Columbia Pictures which starred Don Ameche and Joe Mantegna. He has written and illustrated several children's classics, including *Where the Sidewalk Ends, A Light in the Attic,* and *The Giving Tree.* His plays include *The Crate, Lady or the Tiger, Gorilla* and *Little Feet.* He is also a noted cartoonist and the author of many songs and poems. Most recently, his song *I'm Checking Out Of The Heartbreak Hotel* from the film, *Postcards From The Edge,* was nominated for an Academy Award.

ORIGINAL PRODUCTION

The Trio was first produced at the Ensemble Studio Theatre, in Marathon '98, the 21st Annual Festival of One-Act Plays (Curt Dempster, Artistic Director; Jamie Richards, Executive Producer)in New York City, June, 1998. It was directed by Art Wolff with the following cast:

DAVID. . . . . Laurence Luckinbill
HELENA . . . . Janet Zarish
CLAUDIA . . . . Elizabeth Page
THE TRIO:
    CELLIST. . . . . Joyce Feurring
    MONIQUE. . . . . Suzanne Hevner
    VIOLA. . . . . Patricia McCurdy

CHARACTERS

DAVID

HELENA

CLAUDIA

SETTING

An intimate restaurant.

David sits at restaurant table. He studies musical score, making notes. Behind him a trio plays—three women. Helena enters, surprising David.

HELENA: You should have stayed around another ten minutes—all hell broke loose—Oberman's chair collapsed—ba-boom—You should have seen him—with the bassoon all— *(Laughs.)* And then—then I couldn't find my bow—I mean I looked and I looked. I thought, OK, who's the practical joker?—And then that silly little Natalie Ginsberg says, "Well, are you sure you had one when you came in?" That's her bitchy little way of saying I messed up the second passage of the etude, "Are you sure you had one"—

DAVID: I'm sure it was just a joke—she probably—

HELENA: It *was* no joke—oh—and then Malkovsky says, "Are you accusing *me* of stealing your warped little bow?" "Warped little bow"—I said, my dear man, I am not accusing anyone of anything, I'm just trying to—

DAVID: So...?

HELENA: So—finally—I found it.

DAVID: And it was...?

HELENA: In my case—I'd packed it—in my mad rush to get the hell out of there—I'd packed it and forgotten it—Absent-minded musician—twenty lashes with the baton—Anyway...the performance—

DAVID: Ah, the performance—

(Pause.)

HELENA: So...?

DAVID: So...?

HELENA: What did you think of my—?

DAVID: It was lovely.

HELENA: You hated it.

DAVID: You were brilliant—you are always—

HELENA: Brilliant—lovely—everything but *right*—that's your word—*right*— I do not hear "right"—So...what was not right about it?

DAVID: *(Laughs.)* You missed an entrance in the second movement.

HELENA: Seriously—what was not right?

DAVID: My dear, I am being serious—

HELENA: Don't you my dear me—Not about this. I'll be your dear later...Your muse, your—whatever?—unless...you have other plans— *(Beat.)* You do...you have other plans...Well, then, some other night.

DAVID: Jacobson is in from London. I promised him a decision about February—

HELENA: Well then. I'll see you in March.

DAVID: I meant I have to let him know about a Febru—

HELENA: I know what you meant—I was being bitchy—maybe it's the bitchiness you heard creeping into the second movement. Bitchiness *can* sound a lot like a missed entrance to the untrained ear. But you have such a *trained* ear—what would you do if you lost your hearing? Or if you had some horrible stroke and your right side was—*both* sides— you'd conduct with your teeth—you put that baton between your caps and shake the hell out of—that cellist—she's quite good.

DAVID: Um hum. They're all quite accomplished.

HELENA: There was a group playing when you first brought me here—they were playing Schubert—we drank Crystal champagne—we drank to— music. We danced...La da da da...I think I know her—or I've seen her—is she well known?

DAVID: In their own circles. I imagine.

HELENA: They're quite extraordinary—for a restaurant.

DAVID: They play...competently.

HELENA: That violinist—she looks familiar.

DAVID: It's the melody. It's Beethoven.

HELENA: She looks like somebody I—doesn't she look like someone you know? She's better than I am—really—she's much better than I am.

DAVID: Nonsense.

HELENA: She is—David, her—tone...listen to her—

DAVID: Different, not better. No one is better.

HELENA: Sometimes I think no one is better—and then I think *every*one is better.

DAVID: Have some of this pasta—

HELENA: I know...She looks just like that girl at Tanglewood—who was so taken with you—what was her name?—the one with the red hair?— Marie?—Mona?—Something?

DAVID: May I hum something for you?—May I?— *(He does.)* Well—?

HELENA: What is this, Name That Tune? An aptitude test?

DAVID: None of us are above having our aptitudes tested.

HELENA: And if I guess the tune, I get what's behind curtain number three— all right—Brahms Second Serenade—and I'll take the dishwasher and the trip to Hawaii—will you come with me?...

DAVID: What movement?

HELENA: Second movement.

DAVID: And?

HELENA: *And* the D—in the fourth stanza—was flat...Do I pass?

DAVID: *Now*—was it very flat—or just a *trifle*—off?

HELENA: What's the difference? Flat is flat—what are you trying—

DAVID: *Exactly*—flat is flat—ever, ever so slightly flat is flat—off is off—wrong is wrong.

HELENA: I am wrong. Is that what all this is pointing to?

DAVID: Ever so slightly—yes.

HELENA: I am playing flat.

DAVID: That was the—illustration—you are not flat.

HELENA: I'm *off.*

DAVID: Ever so slightly—you are.

HELENA: Me—*personally?*

DAVID: Not you...your—

HELENA: My *music?* My *music* is *off?*

DAVID: At times.

HELENA: At times.

DAVID: *Tonight.*

HELENA: *Tonight? (Laughs.)* Tonight I played—played as though I—had wings. I—soared—I was—

DAVID: The exposition? The Ravel? Second movement? We were in *G*—the rest of us—in the key of G—where were you?

HELENA: Where was I? I was—

DAVID: *Soaring*—Yes—But where?—an octave higher—looking down possibly—soaring—sailing—on some cloud of your own.

HELENA: I was right.

DAVID: An octave higher—*and*—one measure behind the rest of them.

HELENA: *I?*—Was a measure be—

DAVID: *And—and*—

HELENA: Ah—more "ands."

DAVID: Sunday? The Mendelssohn? The Scherzo? The Scherzo is played in what?

HELENA: The—Scherzo—

DAVID: Is played in...?

HELENA: *(Pause—sigh.)* Three-four.

DAVID: Three-four—and you were playing...?

(She sighs.)

DAVID: ...in one.

HELENA: Three-four. *In one? In one*— *(Music stops. She laughs hysterically.)* Really, David, if you want to attack me, attack my weaknesses—I do have some—my...*articulation* could be crisper—my—balance—but *don't* attack my strengths—my time—my passion—Attack the way I resin my bow—Attack my posture—my...

DAVID: You were playing in one. You were in business for yourself. But to hell with Mendelssohn—what does Mendelssohn know? *And*—speaking of resin— *(He reaches into his pocket, takes out a resin cube and puts it on table in front of her.)* You left this after tonight's performance.

HELENA: It isn't mine.

DAVID: It's yours—You're—forgetting things.

HELENA: It is not mine. It's probably Malkovsky's.

DAVID: It's yours—

HELENA: It is not my—

(David takes earring out of pocket and slams it on table. Helena looks down at it. She picks it up. She puts it on.)

DAVID: May I tell you a story—Are you in the mood for a story? Years ago *(Music starts.)* there was a cellist—there *was* a cellist—and there still *is*— I won't state his name—You'd know it—you—well—he progressed in the usual fashion—prodigy—child prodigy—studied with Borenelle in Paris—then Philadelphia—I won't say which symphony—

HELENA: David, I really don't...

DAVID: Finally a seat in a certain Cleveland ensemble—first chair—and *then*...soloist—He was well received, to say the least—well respected, and relatively well paid—*and* relatively happy—for a while—then what? The pressure?—the celebrity?—it started getting to him—not his technique—not his approach—not his ego—but...something—too much attention?—not enough attention?—In any case, he came to me. It was after an especially...wrenching rendition of the Brahms Four—He was sweating—"Maestro," he said, "Maestro, I am—unfit"—*Unfit?* He had performed brilliantly—or so it seemed...But I was only listening to his music, Helena. I wasn't hearing his heart—beat...and break—I didn't know what each performance was *costing* him—"I'm finished, Maestro," he said—"I am unqualified to play even in a high school marching band. I will never perform again." Well, what could I do? No, I said to *him*— step back—not down—do not step down—step back—"Where?" he asked—Back, I said—back to the comfort, to the joy, the pleasure—take a chair—He was not insulted—he was not shocked—"I don't know if I can even function in a third chair"—Of course you can—I said, step back—He did—I found him a chair in the...a certain midwestern symphony—he performed—he supported—he looked to either side of him—he saw friends—he looked straight ahead, he saw other soloists—

sweating—he did *not* sweat—he played—*play*—that's what we begin doing, isn't it?—We *play* the violin—the *fiddle*—like we *play* hide and seek—we *play*—we *play*—and then as we become skilled—the play becomes skill and the skill becomes—proficiency and the proficiency becomes—*brilliance*—ha ha—and the pressure—to *stay* brilliant—to become *more* brilliant—But what happens to the playing? The childlike playing? You're no longer playing, Helena—You are performing—admirably—but…what?—without joy—You are thinking—you are—

HELENA: I think about *us*—How can I not? When you love someone—how can you help but—

DAVID: Love?…Helena—Love should bring out the best in us—in our art—love should nourish our talent like the rain nourishes a flower—a seed—springing it to life—to full blazing life—colors—petals—leaves—

HELENA: Fading—like a flower—dying—

DAVID: Or a flower blooming—Heartbreak can be *heard*—It makes a beautiful sound—loneliness—it stimulates—practice—we turn to our instrument—for solace—comfort—no, Helena—love is the inspiration—unrequited love is the inspiration—loneliness—pain—think of Beethoven's pain—Satie's pain—Chopin—the etudes are written in blood—how many times did Schumann consider suicide?—daily—moment to moment?—Is suicide the answer? It's *an* answer—

HELENA: Suicide?

DAVID: For some—but only the last answer. First, we try building confidence—Then we try…

HELENA: How can I be confident?—I see you looking at me—seeing what? Nothing—seeing me as an instrument—I want to reach out—to touch your hair—to kiss your—all over—It's an embarrassing thing to say.

DAVID: That is why—when one begins to drift away—when one loses the touch—with the music—

HELENA: I do not lose touch. You will not say that to me—No one can say that to me—I hear what I'm playing. You rattle on about my confidence—as a woman—as a lover? What am I now? Violinist—but what else?— *(She reaches for her violin case and gets up to leave.)* I play—I may not be worth much to you—but I *play.*
(David reaches out to restrain her.)

DAVID: And that is what I want you to do—Helena. You must play—as you did—as a child plays—the cellist I mentioned—do you know what happened to him?—After less than a year in a minor role?—You *know* what happened—Everyone knows what happened. Where is he now?—*Ha*—

and that's where you will be—you will return—healed—refreshed—confident as soloist—as—a woman—rested—emotionally—You shall return in triumph—*I* shall conduct you—with the philharmonic—*with* Yoshahara—I can get him—with Valensky—He'll come out for me—and there you shall be—playing and playing—but playing as you never have before—no, you shall not play music—you shall *be* music—you shall be at one—with me—the orchestra—you shall be *triumphant!*

HELENA: *Monique*—that was her name—the one I replaced—the violinist—She looks exactly li—it *is*—it *is* Monique—*Monique*—

(Monique nods.)

HELENA: Monique—It is Monique—what is she doing here?—Playing in—I knew she was—your type—you favor those tall, willowy—God—Monique—

(Waves again.)

HELENA: They're all tall and willowy—that older one—she looks like that photograph of your— *(She realizes.)* It's them—all of them—all your... You've gathered them all—to...Background?...Background for what? They're playing together—as an ensemble.

DAVID: They *are* an ensemble—they work as an ensemble.

HELENA: Work?

DAVID: The word unsettles you—work—that is what you do when you have no first chair in my—or anyone else's—symphony...Work—from nine to midnight—without temperament—with or without inspiration—whether or not one is in the mood—whether or not the spirit is in one—one *works*—

HELENA: Temperamental—is that what this—operetta is all about?—A setting for you to harp on my temperament—

DAVID: I do not harp—harpists harp—cellists cell—

HELENA: Conductors conduct—what are you conducting? Here—what is this composition?—It's all new to me—what *is* this?

DAVID: This is what it is—*this*.

HELENA: What?

DAVID: This...hysteria—this—

HELENA: This hysteria? This is caring, David. This is love—can you—

DAVID: There is a time and a place for love—for—outbursts—not here—and not—on stage.

HELENA: My music is too passionate for the stage? I—

DAVID: *You*—Not your music—You—and you affect me—because I love you—You affect me—my concentration—to look over the top of my score—and see someone who is interested in you—curious about you—

fascinated but demanding—demanding—the best of you—for their continued fascination—that is inspiring—to one's music—one's spirit—but to look over and see—pleading eyes—tear-filled eyes—*imploring* in the middle of Debussy—imploring—I feel guilty—nervous—distracted—slightly—slightly, ever so slightly—and the slightest distraction becomes the slightest discomfort, becomes the slightest lack of concentration—becomes the slightest incommunication—becomes the slightest *flaw*—and I will not have the *slightest* fucking flaw—

HELENA: So my love...is killing the music.

DAVID: You—"love" is killing *me*—*I* am killing the music. I look out and see that— *(Face.)* and I—lose...connection—I'm—lost—and if *I'm* lost, where are we all?—Where are you?

HELENA: I am out there, David, I am playing.

DAVID: Playing an octave higher—playing in one.

HELENA: I am *playing.*

DAVID: You are not playing what's here— *(Notes.)*

HELENA: What's *here?*—black little dots on white paper? Fuck what's *(She crumples page.)* here— *(She throws it at him.)* What's *here*— *(She points to her heart.)* what's coming from *here?*

DAVID: What seems to be coming from here is...

HELENA: Yes?

DAVID: Unacceptable.

HELENA: Unacceptable. *(Pause.)* And?

DAVID: What I advise—what I suggest is a—stepping back.

HELENA: To—Seattle?...Minneapolis? Where? With them?

DAVID: That is beneath you—they are musicians, goddammit—Are you so grand—so—dignified—that you can only be supported and never support? Can you support?—Can you humbly—step back?

HELENA: You...you—couldn't just—a woman...two—three women...even you—to just throw them away like some—

DAVID: I didn't throw them away. I don't throw people away.

HELENA: What then—to just use them?

DAVID: Use?

HELENA: What then—not *use?*

DAVID: To place—safely—to allow them to continue to play—while—

HELENA: Play?

DAVID: Are they not playing?

HELENA: What?—Background music—for your—little...

DAVID: *Music*—goddammit—background—foreground—don't be so damned concerned about what ground you're on or you'll be on no ground at all.

HELENA: *No* ground?

DAVID: You don't believe me? Then go find another seat in another orchestra—of your choosing—you'll have no trouble—Marlanoff would snap you up in a second—Trilini—Orosco—they'd drool to have you—You can have any seat you choose—any maestro you—

HELENA: I don't want a new maestro. I want you—I want to—

DAVID: Then show me—show me—take the chair I assign you—first or fifth or out in the hall or in the ladies room—in Minneapolis or Timbucktoo—or with *them*. If you find it—advantageous—to your best interests—to play for me—ever again—you will take the seat that's— available to you. *(He glances at wristwatch.)*

(Helena stands—looks at trio—looks at him—picks up her instrument— walks to trio—they make room—she sits—she adjusts to group—David turns back to his notations. Claudia enters.)

CLAUDIA: Am I—late?—I was just—

DAVID: Ah—you're here—please sit down—

(He waves her to seat. Meanwhile, Helena is adjusting to group—one shares music with her—one whispers for a moment with her.)

DAVID: All right—Claudia? Claudia—You're going to play for me—

(She squeals—he silences her with a wave.)

DAVID: You will play what I say—when I say and how I say—*Eh?* Eh?

(Claudia nods. Helena is now playing with the group.)

DAVID: Together all of us, dependent upon each other—all sharing a common purpose. And that is…? Perfection, only musical perfection, and we'll never achieve it, Claudia, but we will not be deterred, and we will not be distracted and we will come as close as is humanly and artistically possible to that perfection— *(He picks up crumpled paper.)* This…is not the music, Claudia, the music is in here— *(Heart.)* We open Friday with the Bartok concerto and the Mozart Divertimento.

(She takes them—he pulls them out of her hand.)

DAVID: You know them—this is not a time for study—this is a moment of— what?—celebration— *(He pours champagne for her.)* To…the music?

CLAUDIA: To—music—

(They drink.)

DAVID: Good?

CLAUDIA: Perfect…Thank you…It's a lovely place— *(She glances at quartet.)* A lovely group…

(Lights fade.)

END OF PLAY

The Hundred Penny Box

BY BARBARA SUNDSTROM

from the Newbery Honor Book
The Hundred Penny Box by Sharon Bell Mathis

TO THE MEMORY OF SHARON'S MATERNAL GRANDPARENTS,
RICHARD FRAZIER, SR. AND HIS WIFE, MARY FRAZIER,
AND TO SHARON'S BROTHER, JOHN W. BELL.

AND TO THE MEMORY OF MY GRANDMOTHER, CARRIE BECKER BROWN,
TO MY FAMILY: DAVID, ERICA, ROBERT, ANN, CARLY,
TO SHARON BELL MATHIS
AND TO THE PRECIOUS LORD
WHO "TAKES MY HAND AND LEADS ME ON."

THE AUTHOR

Barbara Sundstrom made her off-Broadway debut with *The Hundred Penny Box* and would like to thank Sharon Bell Mathis and The Ensemble Studio Theatre for this extraordinary opportunity. Her other professionally produced plays include *Gideon* and *Joseph and The Madras Plaid Jacket,* originally presented at A. D. Players, Houston, Texas, and *Doc in the Box,* a semifinalist in New York City's Lamia Ink One Page Play Contest. Ms. Sundstrom holds a M.A. in Communications from the University of Houston and is a member of The Dramatists Guild.

ORIGINAL PRODUCTION

The Hundred Penny Box was originally presented by The Ensemble Studio Theatre, New York, New York, Curt Dempster, Artistic Director. Jamie Richards, Executive Producer. It was directed by Woodie King, Jr. with the following cast:

MICHAEL JOHN JEFFERSON . . . . Chad Tucker
DEWBET THOMAS . . . . Sarallen
RUTH JEFFERSON . . . . Denise Burse
JOHN JEFFERSON . . . . Kim Sullivan

AUTHOR'S NOTE

I remember my grandmother...I liked to brush her hair because she would tell me stories of days past, of faces I'd never seen but were a part of me—of who I was—of who I was to become...I remember my grandmother.

—Barbara Sundstrom

CHARACTERS

MICHAEL JOHN JEFFERSON: An African-American boy, age eight to ten
DEWBET THOMAS: Michael's great-great aunt, age one hundred
RUTH JEFFERSON: Michael's mother, age early thirties
JOHN JEFFERSON: Michael's father, age middle thirties

SETTING

The interior of a small A-frame house

TIME

1974

SET DESCRIPTION

The primary level of the small house contains a kitchen, stage right, and the master bedroom, stage left. Above the kitchen and master bedroom is an attic bedroom that has a dormer window, center, with a bureau below the window-sill. On the bureau sits a very large, battered, old wooden box. A flight of stairs leads from the attic bedroom to the main floor. At the foot of the stairs, a door leads to the basement.

SCENE I

Setting: The kitchen, stage right, of the small frame house. There is a table in the center of the kitchen. A stairway, center stage, leads to the attic bedroom. At rise: Aunt Dew and Michael sit at the table, eating ice cream. Ruth stands at the sink, rinsing dishes. Michael, finishing his last bite, bolts up the stairs.

AUNT DEW: John...

RUTH: He's Mike, Aunt Dew. His name is Michael. John's name is John. His name is Michael.

(Aunt Dew does not reply. Ruth pours herself a cup of coffee and crosses to the table. Aunt Dew slowly eats her ice cream.)

RUTH: I rode all the way to Mama Dee's to get some decent ice cream...

(Aunt Dew continues eating.)

RUTH: ...Mama Dee said, "The ice cream be melted 'fore you get home..." *(No reply.)* ...so I took a cab back... You finished? I just clear off these dishes.

(Aunt Dew finishes the last of her ice cream and rises.)

RUTH: Here, let me help you.

AUNT DEW: I been getting up from a chair a long time. Can still do it.

(Ruth lets her go as Aunt Dew crosses to the stairs and starts slowly up, holding the railing. Ruth watches after her as the lights fade. Blackout. End of scene.)

SCENE II

Setting: The downstairs master bedroom, stage left. Moonlight shines upstairs through the attic dormer window, partially lighting Michael's bed. At rise: John and Ruth are in the master bedroom. Michael sits in the moonlight on his bed in the attic bedroom. Aunt Dew sleeps in her bed in the room with Michael.

RUTH: She won't even look at me—won't call my name, nothing. She doesn't like me. I know it. I can tell. I do everything I can to make her comfortable...

(Michael creeps partially down the stairs to listen.)

RUTH: ...I rode half the way across this city—all the way to Mama Dee's—

to get some homemade ice cream, some decent ice cream. Mama Dee said, "The ice cream be melted 'fore you get home." So I took a cab back and made her lunch and gave her the ice cream. I sat down at the table and tried to drink my coffee—I mean, I wanted to talk to her, say something. But she sat there and ate that ice cream and looked straight ahead at the wall and never said nothing to me. She talks to Mike and if I come around she even stops talking sometime...

(John wraps his arms around Ruth. She cries softly. Michael moves down the stairs a little, straining to hear.)

RUTH: ...I care about her. But she's making me miserable in my own house.

JOHN She's a one-hundred-year-old lady, baby. And when I didn't have nobody, she was there. Look here—after Big John and Junie drowned, she gave me a home. I didn't have one. I didn't have nothing. No mother, no father, no nobody. Nobody but her. I've loved her all my life. Like I love you. And that tough beautiful boy we made—standing right outside the door and listening for all he's worth—and he's supposed to be in his room 'sleep...

(Michael bolts up the stairs and into his bed.)

JOHN: Hold tight, Ruth. She knows we want her. She knows it. And baby, baby—sweet woman, you doing fine. Everything you doing is right.

(John wraps his arms around Ruth as the lights fade. Blackout. End of scene.)

SCENE III

Setting: The attic bedroom, daylight. The top branches of a tree are visible through the dormer window and a large, old, battered wooden box sits on the bureau beneath the windowsill. At rise: Aunt Dew sits in the rocking chair, and Michael is on his bed watching her. Ruth works downstairs in the master bedroom and the kitchen, folding clothes and cleaning house. Aunt Dew rocks, humming the melody to the hymn, "Precious Lord, Take My Hand." Michael crosses to the box, running his hand across the top.

MICHAEL: Aunt Dew...

(Aunt Dew continues humming.)

MICHAEL: ...Can we play with the hundred penny box?

AUNT DEW: *(Singing.) Precious Lord—*

MICHAEL: Aunt Dew! Let's count the pennies out.

AUNT DEW: *Take my hand—*

MICHAEL: Aunt Dew!

AUNT DEW: *Lead me on—*

> (*Michael sighs. He lifts the box from the bureau, placing it gently on the floor. He crosses to Aunt Dew, cupping his hands around her ear.*)

MICHAEL: Aunt Dew!

> (*Aunt Dew stops rocking, looks at Michael, then begins rocking and singing again where she left off.*)

AUNT DEW: *Let me stand—*

> (*Michael crosses back to the box. He picks up the heavy box, looks at Aunt Dew, then starts down the stairs, carrying the box.*)

AUNT DEW: *I am weak. I am worn—*

> (*Michael enters the kitchen.*)

RUTH: What's wrong?

> (*Michael hesitates, then sits at the kitchen table, holding the large box and staring at the floor.*)

AUNT DEW: *Take my hand, precious Lord, lead me home—*

RUTH: Oh…Give me that thing. That goes today! Soon as Aunt Dew's asleep, that goes in the furnace!

MICHAEL: *(Leaping up.)* You can't take the hundred penny box! I'll tell Daddy if you take it and burn it up in the furnace like you burned up all the rest of Aunt Dew's stuff!

> (*Ruth starts to cross to him, then stops.*)

RUTH: *(Softly.)* Michael, honey, Aunt Dew's like a child. She's like you. Thinks she needs a whole lot of stuff she really doesn't. I'm not taking her pennies—you know I wouldn't take her pennies. I'm just getting rid of that big old ugly wooden box always under foot.

MICHAEL: No!

RUTH: Mike, did you say no to me?

MICHAEL: I mean…Aunt Dew won't go to sleep if she doesn't see her box. Can I take it back and then you can let her see it? And when she goes to sleep, you can take it.

RUTH: Go put it back in her room then. I'll get it later.

MICHAEL: Okay.

> (*Michael carries the heavy box upstairs. He sets it on the floor and sits on it, staring at Aunt Dew.*)

AUNT DEW: John-boy.

MICHAEL: Yes, Aunt Dew.

AUNT DEW: Put my music on.

(Michael reaches under his bed, pulling out his small record player and plugging it in the wall.)

AUNT DEW: Get mine. My own Victrola, the one your father give me.

MICHAEL: Momma threw it out. It was broken.

AUNT DEW: Your momma gonna throw me out soon.

MICHAEL: Momma can't throw people out.

AUNT DEW: Put my music on, boy. And be quick about it.

MICHAEL: Okay.

(Michael pulls out a small chipped record hidden in a bureau drawer and places it on the record player. A lady's voice sings, "Precious Lord, Take My Hand." Michael turns it down low. Aunt Dew hums along then stands and begins swaying to the music. Michael sits on his bed, watching her. Aunt Dew slowly swings her arms from side to side, holding her skirt out, dancing and singing with the music.)

AUNT DEW: Get up, John-boy, and move with me. Move with Dewbet Thomas!

MICHAEL: I don't feel like dancing.

(When the song ends, Michael plays the record again as Aunt Dew sings and hums along, "dancing" to the music.)

MICHAEL: Aunt Dew, where will you put your hundred pennies if you lose your hundred penny box?

AUNT DEW: When I lose my hundred penny box, I lose me.

MICHAEL: I mean maybe you need something better than an old cracked up, wacky-dacky box with the top broken.

AUNT DEW: Them's my years in that box. That's me in that box.

MICHAEL: Can I hide the hundred penny box, Aunt Dew?

(Aunt Dew stops dancing and studies Michael.)

AUNT DEW: No, don't hide my hundred penny box! Leave my hundred penny box right alone. Anybody takes my hundred penny box takes me.

MICHAEL: Just in case. Just in case Momma puts it in the furnace when you go to sleep like she puts all your stuff in the furnace in the basement.

AUNT DEW: What your momma name?

MICHAEL: Oh, no. You keep on forgetting Momma's name.

AUNT DEW: Hush, John-boy. *(Aunt Dew sits back down in the rocking chair, placing a quilt over her legs.)*

MICHAEL: You keep on forgetting.

AUNT DEW: I don't.

MICHAEL: You do; you keep on forgetting!

AUNT DEW: Do I forget to play with you when you worry me to death to play?

(Michael doesn't answer.)

AUNT DEW: Do I forget to play when you want?

MICHAEL: No.

AUNT DEW: Okay. What your momma name? Who's that in my kitchen?

MICHAEL: Momma's name is Ruth, but this isn't your house. Your house is in Atlanta. We went to get you and now you live with us.

AUNT DEW: Ruth. *(Aunt Dew studies Michael silently.)* You John's baby. Look like John just spit you out.

MICHAEL: That's my father.

AUNT DEW: My great-nephew. Only one ever care about me.

(Aunt Dew sits quietly, rocking in her chair. Michael turns off the record player and returns the record to its hiding place in the bureau drawer.)

AUNT DEW: *(Pointing out the window.)* See that tree out there? Didn't have no puny-looking trees like that near my house. Dewbet Thomas—that's me, and Henry Thomas—that was my late husband, had the biggest, tallest, prettiest trees and the widest yard in all Atlanta. And John, that was your daddy, like it most because he was city, and my five sons, Henry, Jr., and Truke and Latt and the twins—Booker and Jay—well, it didn't make them no never mind because it was always there. But when my oldest niece Junie and her husband—we called him Big John— brought your daddy down to visit every summer, they couldn't get the suitcase in the house good before he was climbing up and falling out the trees. We almost had to feed him up them trees!

MICHAEL: Aunt Dew, we have to hide the box.

AUNT DEW: Junie and Big John went out on that water and I was feeling funny all day. Didn't know what. Just feeling funny. I told Big John, I said, "Big John, that boat old. Nothing but a piece a junk." But he fooled around and said, "We taking it out." I looked and saw him and Junie on that water. Then it wasn't nothing. Both gone. And the boat turned over, going downstream. Your daddy, brand-new little britches on, just standing there looking, wasn't saying nothing. No hollering. I try to give him a big hunk of potato pie. But he just looking at me, just looking and standing. Wouldn't eat none of that pie. Then I said, "Run get Henry Thomas and the boys." He looked at me and then he looked at that water. He turned 'round real slow and walked toward the west field. He never run. All you could see was them stiff little britches—red they was—moving through the corn. Bare-waisted, he was. When we found the boat later, he took it clean apart—what was left of it—every plank, and pushed it back in that water. I watched him. Wasn't a piece left of that boat. Not a splinter.

MICHAEL: Aunt Dew, where can we hide the box.

AUNT DEW: What box?

MICHAEL: The hundred penny box.

AUNT DEW: We can't hide the hundred penny box and if she got to take my hundred penny box—she might as well take me.

MICHAEL: We have to hide it.

AUNT DEW: No—*we* don't. It's *my* box.

MICHAEL: It's *my* house. And I said we have to hide it.

AUNT DEW: How you going to hide a house, John?

MICHAEL: Not the house! Our hundred penny box.

AUNT DEW: It's *my* box.

MICHAEL: Suppose Momma takes it when you go to sleep?

(Aunt Dew stops rocking and stares at Michael.)

AUNT DEW: Like John just spit you out. Go on count them pennies, boy. Less you worry me in my grave if you don't. Dewbet Thomas's hundred penny box. Dewbet Thomas a hundred years old and I got a penny to prove it—each year.

(Michael picks up the box and carries it to Aunt Dew, setting it at her feet and sitting down on the floor. Opening the top, Michael reaches in to take out the small roseprint cloth sack filled with pennies. Emptying the sack, Michael picks up the first penny.)

AUNT DEW: Why you want to hide my hundred penny box?

MICHAEL: …To play.

AUNT DEW: Play now. Don't hide my hundred penny box. I got to keep looking at my box and when I don't see my box I won't see me neither.

(Michael drops the first penny back in the sack, counting.)

MICHAEL: One…

AUNT DEW: 1874. Year I was born. Slavery over. Black men in Congress running things. They was in charge. It was the Reconstruction…

(Michael keeps counting as Aunt Dew talks.)

MICHAEL: …eleven, twelve…

AUNT DEW: …Things look better for Black folk—Freedmen they call us—Freedman's Bureau started schools and colleges. Black folk getting an education. Things look better…for awhile…

MICHAEL: …twenty-six, twenty-seven…

(Aunt Dew taps Michael.)

AUNT DEW: Stop right there, boy. You know what that penny means?

MICHAEL: You tell me.

AUNT DEW: 19 and 01. I was twenty-seven years. Birthed my twin boys.

Hattie said, "Dewbet, you got two babies." I asked Henry Thomas, I said, "Henry Thomas, what them boys look like?"…

(Ruth walks up the stairs during the following conversation. Michael continues counting.)

MICHAEL: …thirty-eight, thirty-nine…

AUNT DEW: …He said, "Why, Dew baby, they look like each other." I said, "Give me them babies. You're right, Henry Thomas. They look just like each other." Hattie said, "Dewbet, ain't no way you tell them two babies apart." I said, "Hattie, a momma always knows her babies…"

MICHAEL: …fifty-five, fifty—

(Aunt Dew grabs Michael's arm, stopping him. Ruth arrives unnoticed at the top of the stairs. Sometime during the following speech Michael notices his mother, Ruth.)

AUNT DEW: …19 and 30. Depression. Henry Thomas, that was my late husband, died. Died after he put the fifty-six penny in my box. He had the double pneumonia and no decent shoes and he worked too hard. Said he was going to sweat the trouble out his lungs. Couldn't do it. Same year I sewed that fancy dress for Rena Coles. She want a hundred bows all over that dress. I was sewing bows and tying bows and twisting bows and cursing all the time. Was her fourth husband and she want a dress full of bow-ribbons. Henry the one started that box, you know. Put the first thirty-one pennies in it for me and it was my birthday. After fifty-six, I put them all in myself.

RUTH: Aunt Dew, time to go to bed.

AUNT DEW: Now, I'm not sleepy. John-boy and me just talking. Why you don't call him John? Look like John just spit him out. Why you got to call that boy something different from his daddy?

(Ruth crosses to the bureau, putting the clothes she is carrying in the drawer. She opens the dormer window.)

RUTH: We'll get some fresh air in here. And then, Aunt Dew, you can take your nap better and feel good when you wake up.

(Ruth reaches down to take the bag of pennies from Michael but he holds tightly to the bag.)

AUNT DEW: I'm not sleepy. This child and me just talking.

RUTH: I know. But we're just going to take our nap anyway.

AUNT DEW: I got a long time to sleep and I ain't ready now. Just leave me sit here in this little narrow piece a room. I'm not bothering nobody.

RUTH: Nobody said you're bothering anyone but as soon as I start making that meat loaf, you're going to go to sleep in your chair and fall out again and hurt yourself and John'll wonder where I was and say I was on the telephone and that'll be something all over again.

AUNT DEW: Well, I'll sit on the floor and if I fall, I'll be there already and it won't be nobody's business but my own.

(Ruth takes the sack of pennies from Michael, places it inside the box and shuts the lid.)

RUTH: Michael, go out the room, honey, and let Momma help Aunt Dew into bed.

(Michael starts to leave but hesitates at the doorway.)

AUNT DEW: I been putting Dewbet Thomas to bed a long time and I can still do it.

RUTH: I'll just help you a little.

(Ruth sees Michael in the doorway.)

RUTH: Why are you looking like that? If you want to play, go in my room. Play there or in the kitchen. And don't go bothering Aunt Dew. She needs her rest.

(As Ruth gets Aunt Dew's bed ready, Michael starts slowly down the stairs. Halfway down he speeds up, rushing down to the basement door. Looking to see if his mother is coming, Michael quietly opens the door to the basement. Ruth continues to get Aunt Dew settled for her nap upstairs as Michael sneaks quietly back in the kitchen from the basement, looks for his mother, then crosses to his parents' downstairs bedroom. Ruth comes downstairs to the kitchen and Michael sneaks quietly but excitedly upstairs.)

MICHAEL: *(Quietly.)* Aunt Dew?

(Aunt Dew cries softly but does not answer.)

MICHAEL: Aunt Dew. It's me. Michael. *(Michael pulls the covers back a little from Aunt Dew's face. Softly.)* Aunt Dew, don't cry... *(Michael walks down the stairs to the kitchen where Ruth is preparing supper.)*

MICHAEL: Aunt Dew's crying.

RUTH: That's all right. Aunt Dew's all right.

MICHAEL: She's crying real hard.

RUTH: When you live long as Aunt Dew's lived, honey—sometimes you just cry. She'll be all right.

MICHAEL: She's not sleepy. You shouldn't make her go to sleep if she doesn't want to. Daddy never makes her go to sleep.

RUTH: You say you're not sleepy either, but you always go to sleep.

MICHAEL: Aunt Dew's bigger than me.

RUTH: She needs her naps.

MICHAEL: Why?

RUTH: Michael, go play please. I'm tired and I'm busy and she'll hear your noise and never go to sleep.

MICHAEL: *(Raising his voice.)* She doesn't have to if she doesn't want! We were just playing and then you had to come and make her cry!

RUTH: Without a nap, she's irritable and won't eat. She has to eat. She'll get sick if she doesn't eat.

MICHAEL: You made her cry!

RUTH: *(Quietly, controlled.)* Michael John Jefferson. If you don't get away from me and stop that yelling and stop that screaming and leave me alone—!

(Michael stands looking at his mother, then turns to leave.)

RUTH: Michael, wait.

(Michael stops but does not turn around. Ruth crosses to him and puts her arms around him, hugging him. Ruth turns Michael around to face her.)

RUTH: Mike, I'm going to give Aunt Dew that tiny mahogany chest your daddy made in a wood shop class when he was a teenager. It's really perfect for that little sack of pennies and when she sees it on that pretty dresser scarf she made—the one I keep on her dresser—she'll like it just as well as that big old clumsy box. She won't even miss that big old ugly thing!

MICHAEL: The hundred penny box isn't even bothering you! *(Michael turns and pulls away from his mother.)* You don't even care about Aunt Dew's stuff.

RUTH: *(Quietly.)* Mike... Do you remember that teddy bear you had? The one with the crooked head? We could never sit him up quite right because of the way you kept him bent all the time. You'd bend him up while you slept with him at night and bend him up when you hugged him, played with him. Do you remember that, Mike?...You wouldn't let us touch that teddy bear. I mean it was all torn up and losing its stuffing all over the place. And your daddy wanted to get rid of it and I said, "No. Mike will let us know when he doesn't need that teddy bear anymore." So you held onto that teddy bear and protected it from all kinds of monsters and people. Then, one day, you didn't play with it anymore. I think it was when little Corky moved next door.

MICHAEL: Corky's not little.

RUTH: I'm sorry. Yes—Corky's big. He's a very big boy. But Corky wasn't around when you and I cleaned up your room a little while back. We got rid of a lot of things so that Aunt Dew could come and be more comfortable. That day, you just tossed that crooked teddy bear on top of the heap and never even thought about it—

MICHAEL: I *did* think about it.

RUTH: But you knew you didn't need it anymore…But it's not the same with Aunt Dew. She will hold onto everything that is hers—just to hold onto them. She will hold them tighter and tighter, and she will not go forward and try to have a new life. This is a new life for her, Mike. You must help her have this new life and not just let her go backward to something she can never go back to. Aunt Dew does not need that huge, broken, half-rotten wooden box that you stumble all over the house with—just to hold one tiny little sack of pennies.

MICHAEL: I don't stumble around with it.

(Ruth kisses the top of Michael's head.)

RUTH: You're the one that loves that big old box, Mike. I think that's it.

MICHAEL: All Aunt Dew wants is her hundred penny box. That's the only thing—

RUTH: And all you wanted was that teddy bear.

(Michael pushes away from Ruth's embrace.)

MICHAEL: You can't burn it. You can't burn any more of Aunt Dew's stuff. You can't take the hundred penny box. I said you can't take it!

RUTH: Okay.

(Michael starts up the stairs. Ruth follows after Michael.)

RUTH: No, Mike. Don't go in there now.

MICHAEL: I am.

(Ruth grabs Michael by the arm, taking him to the master bedroom, and sits him down.)

RUTH: You're as stubborn as your father. Everything your way or else! Just sit there and don't move until I tell you!

(Ruth returns to the kitchen. Michael sneaks up the stairs to the attic bedroom. He tiptoes over to Aunt Dew in her bed.)

MICHAEL: Aunt Dew?

AUNT DEW: What you want, John-boy?

MICHAEL: I'm sorry Momma's mean to you.

AUNT DEW: Ain't nobody mean to Dewbet Thomas—cause Dewbet Thomas ain't mean to nobody. Your Momma Ruth. She move around and do what she got to do. First time I see her, I say, "John, she look frail but she ain't." He said, "No, she ain't frail." I make out like I don't see her all the time. But she know I see her. If she think I don't like her that ain't the truth. Dewbet Thomas like everybody. But me and her can't talk like me and John talk—cause she don't know all what me and John know.

MICHAEL: You don't have to sleep if you don't want to.

AUNT DEW: I been 'sleep all day, John.

MICHAEL: You haven't been 'sleep all day. You've been sitting in your chair and talking to me and then you were dancing to your record and then we were counting pennies and we got to fifty six and then Momma came.

AUNT DEW: Where my hundred penny box?

MICHAEL: I got it.

AUNT DEW: Where you got it?

MICHAEL: Right here by the bed.

AUNT DEW: Watch out while I sleep.

MICHAEL: Okay.

AUNT DEW: Look like John just spit you out.

(Michael turns away.)

AUNT DEW: Turn around. Let me look at you.

(Michael turns around to look at Aunt Dew.)

AUNT DEW: John!

MICHAEL: It's me. Michael.

(Michael crosses to the box, sitting on it.)

AUNT DEW: Come here so I can see you.

(Michael doesn't move.)

AUNT DEW: Stubborn like your daddy. Don't pay your Aunt Dew no never mind.

(Michael doesn't move.)

AUNT DEW: Go on back and do your counting out my pennies. Start with fifty-seven—where you left off. 19 and 31. Latt married that school-teacher. We roasted three pigs. Just acting the fool, everybody. Latt give her a pair of yellow shoes for her birthday. Walked off down the road one evening just like you please, she did. Had on them yellow shoes. Rode a freight train clean up to Chicago. Left his food on the table and all his clothes ironed. Six times she come back and stay for a while and then go again. Truke used to say, "Wouldn't be my wife." But Truke never did marry nobody. Only thing he care about was that car. He would covered it with a raincoat when it rained, if he could.

MICHAEL: First you know me, then you don't.

AUNT DEW: Michael John Jefferson what your name is. Should be plain John like your daddy and your daddy's daddy—'stead of all this new stuff.

Name John and everybody saying "Michael." Come here, boy. Come here close. Let me look at you. Got a head full of hair.

(Michael gets up and crosses to Aunt Dew's bed.)

AUNT DEW: Get closer.

(Michael moves closer.)

AUNT DEW: Turn these covers back little more. This little narrow piece a room don't have the air the way my big house did.

MICHAEL: I took a picture of your house.

AUNT DEW: My house bigger than your picture. Way bigger.

MICHAEL: Tell me about the barn again.

AUNT DEW: Dewbet and Henry Thomas had the biggest, reddest barn in all Atlanta, G-A.

MICHAEL: And the swing Daddy broke.

AUNT DEW: Did more pulling it down than he did swinging.

MICHAEL: Tell me about the swimming pool.

(Michael touches Aunt Dew's face. She is quiet for a moment.)

AUNT DEW: Wasn't no swimming pool. I done told you was a creek. Plain old creek. And your daddy like to got bit by a cottonmouth.

MICHAEL: Don't go to sleep, Aunt Dew. Let's talk.

AUNT DEW: I'm tired, John.

MICHAEL: I can count the pennies all the way to the end if you want me to.

AUNT DEW: Go head and count.

MICHAEL: When your hundred and one birthday comes, I'm going to put in the new penny like you said.

AUNT DEW: Yes, John.

(Michael reaches up and touches Aunt Dew's eyes.)

MICHAEL: I have a good place for the hundred penny box, Aunt Dew.

AUNT DEW: Go way. Let me sleep.

MICHAEL: You wish you were back in your own house, Aunt Dew?

AUNT DEW: I'm going back.

MICHAEL: You sad?

AUNT DEW: Hush, boy.

(Michael crawls up on the bed alongside Aunt Dew. He touches her arms.)

MICHAEL: Are your arms a hundred years old?

AUNT DEW: Um-hm.

(Michael touches Aunt Dew's face.)

MICHAEL: Is your face and your eyes and fingers a hundred years old too?

AUNT DEW: John, I'm tired. Don't talk so.

MICHAEL: How do you get to be a hundred years old?

AUNT DEW: *(Sleepily.)* First you have to have a hundred penny box.

MICHAEL: Where you get it from?

AUNT DEW: Somebody special got to give it to you... *(Aunt Dew hands Michael the hundred penny box.)* ...And soon as they give it to you, you got to be careful less it disappear. *(Aunt Dew crosses to her rocking chair and sits. Singing.)* Precious Lord—

MICHAEL: Aunt Dew? *(Michael crosses to Aunt Dew.)*

AUNT DEW: *Take my hand—*

(Michael holds the box, standing close to her as Aunt Dew sings the rest of the hymn.)

AUNT DEW: *(Singing.)* *Lead me on—*

Let me stand—

I am tired, I am weak, I am worn—

Thro' the storm, thro' the night,

Lead me on to the light—

Take my hand, precious Lord, lead me home...

MICHAEL: Aunt Dew ...

(No answer. The lights fade.)

MICHAEL: Aunt Dew...

(Blackout.)

END OF PLAY

Killing Hand

BY DAVID ZELLNIK

FOR MIRIAM,
AND FOR JORDAN

THE AUTHOR

David Zellnik graduated with a BFA in Acting from NYU in 1993, and in a moment of good fortune, soon became one of the founding members of Youngblood, a writer-based group created by Curt Dempster to help foster emerging theatre professionals. He is deeply indebted to both Youngblood and EST, which, for the past five years have provided him with a safe space for new work. He is also proud to be the first member of Youngblood to have a one-act in the Marathon.

David is the author of numerous plays that have been performed in New York, including *Let a Hundred Flowers Bloom, Karmic Thunder, A Litany of Sorrows,* and *Participatory Democracy;* and in Prague, including *Prodigal Son* at the Divadelni Ostrov Theatre Festival. David's fascination with history and politics recently led him to the Nineteenth Century with *City of Dreams,* a musical about the suicide of Crown Prince Rudolf in 1889 Vienna, written in collaboration with his brother, Joseph Zellnik.

Since *Killing Hand,* David is thrilled to have received a commission from the Sloan Foundation for a new play about science, as well as a grant from the New York State Council of the Arts for an adaptation of Kipling's "Just So" Stories, to be premiered at Syracuse Stage.

ORIGINAL PRODUCTION

Killing Hand was first produced at the Ensemble Studio Theatre, in Marathon '98, the 21st Annual Festival of One-Act Plays (Curt Dempster, Artistic Director; Jamie Richards, Executive Producer)in New York City, May, 1998. It was directed by Chris Smith with the following cast:

EVAN . . . . Grant James Varjas
JOHN. . . . . Chris Lutkin
ELENA. . . . . Sylva Kelegian
DICK . . . . Ted Neustadt
JURAJ. . . . . Jason Kolotouros

CHARACTERS

EVAN: Late twenties, early thirties. High strung, intensely verbal, and very funny.

JOHN: Mid to late thirties (though probably looks younger). Evan's boyfriend/husband, the more grounded of the two.

ELENA: Late twenties, early thirties. A Serbian immigrant and proud of it, speaks flawless—if accented—English.

DICK: Mid to late thirties. Elena's husband, easy-going, affable, a good host.

JURAJ: Mid-twenties to late twenties. Elena's younger brother, quiet, clearly out of his element, also he has seen too much of the war in Bosnia. Understands English better than he speaks it. He is missing his left hand.

SETTING

An apartment in Park Slope, Brooklyn—Elena and Dick's—well appointed, modern, a large table set for dinner for five

TIME

The play takes place in the late 1990s

SERBIAN DIALOGUE AND PRONUNCIATION

The Serbo-Croatian translations for this play were done by Amela Baksic. Two important pronunciations for the whole cast are:

1. Juraj is pronounced "YOUR-eye" (accent on the first syllable)
2. Srebrenica is pronounced "SRE-bren-eetsa" (accent on the first syllable)
3. Dusic is pronounced "DOO-sitch"

For those interested in producing the play, Elena and Juraj's ten or so lines of Serbian dialogue can be obtained broken down phonetically line by line. That said, I do think a native speaker/dialect coach is necessary in order to really get the sound of the speech in action.

Lastly, Amela wrote the dialogue in the Bosnian Serb dialect, however I have chosen to write the lines here in Latin letters—as the Croats do (rather than in the Cyrillic alphabet, as the Serbs do) —for readability's sake.

AUTHOR'S NOTE

I am suspicious of notes before a play, so I will just say this: although *Killing Hand* is a work of fiction, the events it describes are unfortunately all too true. The massacre of at least six thousand Muslim men and boys by the Bosnian Serbian troops before the eyes of the UN peacekeeping force (who had declared Srebrenica a "protected" safe haven) has been described as one of the worst atrocities to take place in Europe since WWII. There is certainly a part of me reluctant to admit any fascination with the awfulness of what occurred there, but then I do not trust the desire to look away and ignore it either.

Killing Hand received a top notch production at EST under the smart, scrupulous, theatrically savvy direction of Chris Smith. Also, I know I told the cast this, but here it is in print: you were a dream cast. Thank you guys.

Lastly, there were many people whose criticism and comments proved invaluable for this play, most notably: Chris Smith, Jordan Schildcrout, Curt Dempster, Jamie Richards, and the members of Youngblood.

—David Zellnik

A brief, contemplative moment before the start of the play. In three pools of light we see Dick setting up for drinks at the side bar, Elena, his wife, watching her younger brother Juraj, who sits at a large table set for dinner. Over music, a buzzer sounds, though perhaps the sound is distorted. Elena appears lost in thought, as she stares at her brother. The buzzer sounds again, now more clearly. Dick motions to Elena to get the door, which she does.

ELENA: *(Offstage.)* Welcome, hello!
(At once the mood changes—bright now, festive. A dinner party. Lights reveal an apartment in Park Slope—Elena and Dick's—well-appointed, modern, classy. Music, if there is any, is low, contemporary, suitable for a cocktail party. Enter Evan and John, Americans, a gay couple.)

DICK: Hey, guys. Welcome. Come on in.

JOHN: Hey.

EVAN: So this is Brooklyn.

ELENA: Very funny. Dick take their coats.

DICK: *(A la plantation.)* Yess'm. *(In his own voice.)* I can't remember have you guys ever been here?

EVAN: No. Not since you moved I don't think—

JOHN: *(Whispered.)* Hey Elena, is that Juraj? I got him something.

ELENA: Oh, that's so sweet.

DICK: *(Taking box, guessing what's in the box.)* Champagne?

JOHN: *(A tease.)* Maybe.
(Dick takes their coats.)

ELENA: Juraj? I'd like you to meet our friends over at the university—

JOHN: *(To Dick, about the gift.)* Give it back.

ELENA: —Evan and John.
(Juraj stands, reaches one hand out to John, keeps other hidden.)

JURAJ: *(Awkward English.)* Pleasure.
(Juraj shakes John's, then Evan's hand. When he shakes Evan's hand, Evan has a slight sense of being taken aback, as if, perhaps, he might recognize Juraj from a previous meeting.)

JOHN: Here, this is from both of us.

JURAJ: Thank you. That is very nice. What is it?

JOHN: Well you have to open it.

JURAJ: *(Pauses, considers.)* In a little.
(Juraj looks at Evan. Evan consciously relaxes his own gaze. He places gift, unopened, on a side table.)

DICK: So a drink?

JOHN: Sure.

EVAN: Gimme whatever all the kids are drinking these days…Martinis?

JOHN: Me too. Shaken, not stirred.

EVAN: Jesus John.

JOHN: What?

EVAN: You ruined it. None of the kids would quote James Bond anymore.

JOHN: I'm just an old fogie, baby.

DICK: Remind me to buy you a walker for your next birthday. *(Leaves to get drinks.)*

EVAN: Hi, Juraj. So…How was your trip over? I imagine it had to be a really exhausting flight, right?

JOHN: How do you expect him to understand when you talk so quickly?

ELENA: My brother understands. You don't realize the whole world speaks your crummy language.

EVAN: "Crummy?"

ELENA: I'm kidding. Juraj tell them.

JURAJ: Trip? Trip was fine. I drank a lot. *(That is all he is going to say.)*

EVAN: Well huh.

(Dick re-enters with shaker full of gin, makes drinks at the table. Each in their own time moves to sit down. Conversation flows easily.)

DICK: Two olives and very dry, unless you ask for something different. And you can all sit right down…

JOHN: Oh Elena, I've been meaning to ask you about how your talk went about your getting tenure. Matthews is a treat, huh?

ELENA: Oh the usual, you know. There's no real Slavic Studies Department *still* and I only have two students in my advanced language class which isn't enough and fourteen in my beginner's which is too many. So you can imagine…Maybe if Juraj can help out for a while…

JOHN: *(To Juraj.)* Oh wow, you're a teacher too?

ELENA: *(To John.)* No but it would just be for a while, and if you could give him a recommendation…

JOHN: There's a freeze I think, still. Dick are they hiring anyone new?

DICK: Not in Mathematics that's all I know.

ELENA: Just an idea.

EVAN: So, uh, Juraj, what do you think of New York?

JURAJ: Little slower.

JOHN: You see? I told you you talked too quickly—

JURAJ: It's okay. Big.

EVAN: Where have Dick and your sister taken you?

ELENA: Well he slept all day Tuesday and then yesterday and the day before we went—

JURAJ: Mmmm...Statue of Liberty, Empire State, usual tourist crap.

EVAN: The Statue of Liberty is not tourist crap. *(Hushed, to John.)* Is it?

JOHN: 'Fraid so.

EVAN: I was always scared that was true.

DICK: Oh and Juraj god love him wants to see Miss Saigon.

EVAN: No!

JOHN: Evan *you* saw Miss Saigon. You paid one-hundred dollars to see it.

EVAN: You promised you wouldn't tell.

ELENA: Are you making fun of my brother?

EVAN: Not at all.

ELENA: Because he's had a very hard trip over.

JOHN: *(Slowly.)* So where are you from in Serbia?

ELENA: A city called Banja Luka in the eastern part of Bosnia. You wouldn't know it—

EVAN: Elena, it's the capital now, of course we know. Well, that is, if you consider the Bosnian Serb Republic a real country.

DICK: Oooh. Ev's feeling dangerous tonight.

ELENA: Well now of course it's a real country. There is a government and elections.

EVAN: If you want to call them elections.

JOHN: Ev—

EVAN: *(To Elena.)* Now I remember last week you yourself were ranting—

ELENA: *(Overlapping.)* Ranting?

EVAN: —yes—that all Dayton did was to legitimize ethnic cleansing with fake elections—

ELENA: *(Overlapping.)* I never rant and—Yes of course they *rig* them but China rigs its elections and *it's* a nation, a *"most favored nation"* nation—

DICK: No no no politics, guys, please. A toast. To Juraj.

(They all drink and toast.)

JOHN: So Juraj, uh...how long are you in New York for?

JURAJ: Just a little.

ELENA: *(To John.)* Unless you can help get him a post at the University.

JURAJ: Just for a little. I promise. *(Beat.)* Excuse me. *(Juraj gets up and leaves.)*

ELENA: You know all these questions, it's too much for him right at the start—

JURAJ: *(Offstage.)* Elena fuck you I'm just going to the toilet to wash my hands.

(Beat.)

EVAN: Well you see I think his English is great.

ELENA: Evan, John…I love you both but maybe tonight please don't "just be yourselves"—

EVAN: What do you want us to be?

ELENA: I don't know, *nice.*

DICK: Lena!

ELENA: I'm kidding, look—I need you both to help me, it's… *(Real emotion creeps in.)* it's so difficult seeing him like this.

JOHN: Like what?

ELENA: It's been six years, and it's—well it's— *(Her voice gets soft.)* He's in the city because he needs surgery and he's very sensitive about it so…

DICK: *(Soft to Lena.)* He doesn't want surgery, Lena, he said—

ELENA: Dick—

EVAN: What's wrong?

ELENA: Didn't you notice? His hand, there…how do I say this…there was a grenade in his hand he says and it went off—he won't tell me any more. He just says it went off and his—well you can imagine.

JOHN: Oh god, I'm so sorry.

ELENA: It hasn't healed up right I don't think, and it looks awful, and the medicine over there can be primitive, you know, just primitive.

DICK: She said it, I didn't.

ELENA: *(Hits Dick, playful, but real.)* Well ever since the UN sanctions you nincompoop…

JOHN: *(Who taught her that word?!)* Nincompoop!

ELENA: Before that Serbian hospitals were the envy of the East Bloc.

DICK: Woo hoo.

JOHN: Dick!

(Juraj is standing at the door. Elena realizes this.)

ELENA: But really if you could just try and give him a good word, I know you helped people get positions there before—

JURAJ: What, what are you talking about? *(Silence.)* You're talking about this? *(He lifts his arm and shows them: he pats the end of an arm with sleeve sewn over the end; he has no hand.)*

ELENA: Juraj, nemoj. Molim te. [Juraj, no. Please.]

JURAJ: Sta je? [What?]

ELENA: Samo sedi. Molim te [Just sit down. Please]

JURAJ: Je li se stidis onog sto mi se dogodilo? [Are you ashamed of what happened to me?]

ELENA: Ma nije, nego… [Of course not.]

(Juraj turns to Dick, John, and Evan.)

JURAJ: Okay okay it's fine, you don't need to be scared. Dick. Give me a drink.

DICK: What would you like?

ELENA: No dinner is almost ready and I don't want you drinking this early on.

(Elena and Juraj start to argue in Serbo-Croatian.)

JURAJ: Hoces jednom prestati da igras veliku sestru. Ja sam davno odrastao.[Quit being my big sister for a day, I'm all grown up.]

ELENA: Ma nemoj tako Juraj— [Don't give me that, Juraj—]

JURAJ: Otkako sam dosao samo prigovaras isto ko Mama. [What ever since I arrived here you've been nagging just like mom.]

(Simultaneously.)

ELENA: Kad bi te ona sad mogla videti— [If she could see you right now—]

JURAJ: Dobro, volim, svoje pice pa moze li covek popiti nesto s'vecerom. Mogu li dobiti jedan jebeni viski, ili cu umreti? *(Beat.)* Vidi. Tvoj drug. Evan. Njegova ruka. [Okay so I like my drink, a man is allowed to like his drink at a dinner, okay, so could I please have some fucking scotch or I'll die, okay?— *(Beat.)* Look. Your friend. Evan. His hand.]

(Simultaneously.)

JOHN: Wow. This is fascinating. What are they saying?

DICK: Beats me.

JOHN: *(A joke, to Elena and Juraj, but really to Dick...)* Mom, Dad, please stop fighting...

(At first unbeknownst to all, Evan's hand starts to shake. He tries not to pay attention but it rattles the silverware against his plate.)

ELENA: Evan?

EVAN: What?

ELENA: Your hand is shaking, why?

EVAN: No it's not.

ELENA: Evan?

EVAN: Nothing I was just reminded all of a sudden of this article I read a while back— *(Covers his shaking hand with his other hand, trying to re-orient himself.)* It was in the paper a few weeks ago although maybe it was in the New Yorker and ohmygod John said the funniest thing the night before last.

JOHN: What did I say?

EVAN: We were lying in bed talking about whether we should try and be a power couple or not at the University you know, host parties, sponsor events, have power lunches with power people, and John said, out of nowhere: "Do you think the New Yorker will ever draw a cartoon of us?"

ELENA: That would be a joke.

EVAN: *(Playful.)* Shut up, no I realized it's a perfect New Yorker cartoon right there: Two homos in bed, and the caption reads: "Do you think the New Yorker will ever draw a cartoon of us?" Like making it to them means getting a New Yorker cartoon.

ELENA: Dinner's ready, excuse me. *(Elena gets up, exits.)*

JOHN: Are you okay, sweetie?

EVAN: Yeah I'm fine. *(Beat.)* So Juraj, you don't live in Banja Luka, do you?

DICK: What?

JURAJ: No. I live in little town. Srebrenica. It's in Central Bosnian Serb Republic.

(Beat.)

JOHN: That's weird, Ev...

EVAN: *(Soft.)* You're from Srebrenica?

DICK: Come on, leave the man alone.

EVAN: No it's just—when did you move there?

JURAJ: I don't know, I like not to think of such things.

DICK: Ev maybe you should pop a Xanax you're freaking me out—

EVAN: *(To Dick.)* Do you know what Srebrenica is?

(Elena re-enters with food.)

ELENA: *(Light.)* Evan, Evan, Evan, can I not leave you alone for a minute without you bringing up war atrocities, eh? *(To John.)* Is he like this at home?

JOHN: *(Not serious.)* Like this plus ten.

JURAJ: *(To Evan.)* I'm only in New York a little then I go. It's nice here though.

(Elena places main course dish on table.)

ELENA: So this is a new dish for me—

JOHN: Never try a new dish on company.

ELENA: Fuck you. It's squid ink risotto. *(She starts to ladle food onto plates.)*

DICK: Mmm, Lena this looks great.

JOHN: I wonder who first thought of putting squid ink in food?

DICK: Huh...

JOHN: It's weird right? Squid ink.

DICK: Maybe some squid ink just fell into a pot of risotto: Hey you got your squid ink into my risotto—you got your risotto into my—

ELENA: Dick, *try* it. I want to know how it is.

(They all eat. Evan's hand shaking.)

DICK: Mmmmm. Inky.

JOHN: Ease up, Dick.

EVAN: Juraj did you ever know anyone named Mlatko?

JURAJ: Excuse me?

ELENA: *(A school teacher reprimand.)* Evan...

EVAN: Mlatko. Mlatko Dusic. I'm thinking of this interesting story I read.

JURAJ: You're asking me if I know someone named Mlatko?

ELENA: What? What did I miss in the kitchen?

JOHN: Mlatko...It's a lovely name, you know...

DICK: Mlatko, Slobodan, Draza—Serbians all have the greatest names, don't you think?

ELENA: *(Hitting Dick, lightly.)* Stop fetishizing my culture!

DICK: I am not fetishizing your—Jeez I was kidding—

ELENA: Well excuse me but Americans can all think we are some primitive tribal—

DICK: Elena you cannot possibly—you cannot be sitting here after four years of marriage and possibly suggesting that.

ELENA: I've seen worse.

DICK: Oh Lena spare me okay.

JOHN: *(To Evan.)* Are you sure you're okay, baby?

EVAN: Yeah why?

(Juraj speaks in Serbo-Croatian softly and quickly to Elena.)

JURAJ: Sta to on prica o meni? Pitaj ga sta misli. [What is he trying to say about me? Ask him what he means...]

ELENA: My brother feels you are trying to insinuate something. And your hand is shaking why?

EVAN: No it's not. No I'm fine except I was reading about a Serb from Srebrenica before it fell and he also had no hand and his name was Mlatko so I figured maybe Juraj would know him maybe. I mean Srebrenica is a very small town.

JURAJ: Mlatko... I know some Mlatkos but...

EVAN: Mlatko Dusic. I'm trying to remember more. There was a horrible story about him but you never know if they make these things up.

ELENA: That's true.

EVAN: Wait... *(His hand stops.)* For a moment I—No it's gone. I can't remember it. Damn. *(Beat. Tension at the table subsides.)* I guess I was just wondering if you knew him.

DICK: Evan, Bosnia's huge.

EVAN: I know but Srebrenica isn't—especially with Muslims having been killed, no offense.

ELENA: Serbs killing Muslims how many times must we hear about this?

JOHN: Well they did, Elena.

ELENA: Look you don't have to tell me, I left, okay, I protested Milosevic in front of his apartment, did you?

DICK: Well, be honest, you didn't really *protest*.

ELENA: Of course we did Dick. We said "Slobodan—We like everybody"

DICK: For about ten minutes and then left. I mean that's what you told me.

ELENA: It was dangerous.

JOHN: You know Lena, we have *real* protests in America.

ELENA: Ohhhhh, please tell.

JOHN: When I was in Act-Up we closed down the stock market, and Ev, I believe, threw red paint on the president—

EVAN: Uh, the president of Columbia University but—

DICK: Enemy University. Go you!

EVAN: *(Nostalgic.)* Yes…*Rage*…I miss it too.

ELENA: *(Teasing almost.)* You Americans and get one disease and it's endless—

JOHN: Elena!

ELENA: I'm kidding, I know it was awful.

JOHN: Is awful.

ELENA: But not for you personally.

EVAN: Well, straight Serbian woman, it all depends how you define the public impact of a disease.

ELENA: No more definitions, please. Can we eat, yes? I cooked all day…

DICK: Mmm, mmm, mmm, it's good, Lena—

EVAN: You know I have this theory Elena, tell me what you think, as a foreigner.

ELENA: I'm a permanent resident.

EVAN: Whatever. I think Americans have become terribly afraid of disagreement, like it's all "Let's agree to disagree" and "There's two sides to every issue" which leads to, you know, straight to the notion that all points of view have equal merit which, you know, ends up with Holocaust deniers saying on *Nightline*, "What, are they afraid of just letting people hear the *other side?*"

ELENA: No no Evan—it's just that you Americans all think you are going to *learn* something if you get both sides sitting and talking, ignoring all the *posturing* that goes on and, and, the *systemic structural iniquities* that are brought to the—Anyway…

JURAJ: I was not there when they did those things. *(Beat. Silence.)* In Srebrenica.

DICK: What things?

ELENA: Dick.

JURAJ: When they killed the Muslims. I was not there.

(Silence. Evan's hand starts to shake again.)

EVAN: Ah yes. Now I remember the article. It's a really good story. Very disturbing. I think we need wars to have good stories these days.

DICK: Ah the crisis of modern fiction.

EVAN: The guy who wrote it was clearly bucking for a Pulitzer. He sets the scene: The Serbs—the Bosnian Serb Militias—come into Srebrenica, which was supposed to be a UN protected safe haven but the UN just let the Serbs come in, with no opposition. A total abdication of responsibility. They let the Serbs come in and collect all the Muslims' weapons, because the Serbs said it was just "preventative." So the UN did nothing.

Then at night, they came back and all the Muslim men and boys were taken away, ostensibly to this local school where they were going to be held as—the Serbs said—as a "precaution."

ELENA: Evan, I love you but stop, please.

JURAJ: No I am curious. Please. What do you get told over here?

EVAN: Well I'll tell you. I can't remember all the details…but this Mlatko fellow was with his wife when they started to round the Muslims up—

JURAJ: What was his wife's name?

EVAN: I don't know.

ELENA: Evan—

EVAN: Anyway so he left to go help the Militias. And what his job was, was to go around and find all the Muslim men and boys hiding in attics, basements, their mothers' arms, *et cetera,* and what he said to their families when he found them was: "Don't worry, we are sending your boys to Turkey now, and after they get there, they will send for you."

DICK: God that's awful.

EVAN: Oh it gets better. You see Mlatko had this Muslim neighbor—who got shot, I guess—and this neighbor had a son.

Late that night, this boy manages to escape from a sports stadium where they're in the process of creating this—you understand—this mass grave. He manages to escape back to his home but he finds that no one is there, so he goes to his neighbor's house, Mlatko's house, and he tells Mlatko these…unbelievable things, things we might say are *indescribable,* but are actually very easy, even for a child, to find the words to describe. And Mlatko says, he starts crying and says: "Why are they killing them? Why aren't they sending them to Turkey? Why? Why are they doing this?"

JOHN: God the poor man.

DICK: The poor man? He rounded up Muslim kids, John.

JOHN: *(To Evan.)* But you said he didn't know, right? He thought—

DICK: I mean we are talking total collaboration on his part.

ELENA: Dick stop, make him stop.

JURAJ: Ne Elena, I want to hear. Please continue.

EVAN: Well…the story…the story in the article: You see Mlatko lets this boy—Ibrahim, I think—sleep at his house, he feeds him, and he says, "Don't worry, you can stay here." And then the next day—after he has done all this—he goes into town and he tells the Serb Commanders there: "There is a little Turkish liar at my house. He must go to Turkey as well."

   And I'm trying to imagine the look on this poor kid's face when they get there, when he realizes what will happen. I mean does he run, does he scream, what? The article says nothing.

   Okay now the coda. This is the Pulitzer part:

   It turns out Mlatko's wife is half Muslim though she never told him. And the reporter asks him where she is—did she get away?—and at first he won't answer, then he asks this guy what happened to his hand—how he lost his hand—and he says a…an incredible answer, he says: "That was my killing hand."

   He says: "My hand is now buried in a mass grave in Srebrenica where my wife is buried." And he says: "Also my heart is like a mass grave" he said this, he said: "My heart has become a mass grave."

DICK: *(Pause.)* So how did he lose the hand?

ELENA: Dick!

JOHN: Evan?

EVAN: He said when asked again how he lost his hand: "It is buried. I don't know how. I woke up and it was gone." *(Silence. He looks at his own hand, which has stopped shaking. He stares at Juraj.)* How did you lose your hand?

ELENA: Evan!

JOHN: Baby are you okay?

ELENA: Shame!

JOHN: Calm down Elena okay—

ELENA: I invite you here to eat and you tell us ghoulish—you know this is just like you—and I hate to say it—Jewish people to obsess like this about—

JOHN: Elena!

   (Juraj gets up, walks to the bar, fixes himself a scotch.)

ELENA: I didn't bring this up.

DICK: Lena calm down.

JOHN: *(A joke.)* You know when there's a lull in the conversation Evan sometimes thinks he needs to fill in the gaps with horror stories.

EVAN: Please don't talk about me like I'm not here—

DICK: Juraj, I'm sorry, I thought this would be a nice welcome to America sort of thing—

JOHN: Dick calm down, there's no harm—

ELENA: No harm. What, you think every Serb is a murderer. I cannot even have my brother visit for surgery—you know Evan I am sorry about your grandfather but how many times must we hear such things?

JOHN: *(Overlapping.)* Elena that is over the line—

ELENA: My brother has no hand.

JURAJ: Evan—

(All look to Juraj at the bar.)

JURAJ: You seem very curious. I knew people like you in Bosnia. People who looked too long. They don't last.

You say you want to know what someone looks like right before they know they are going to be killed, the moment they are sure? Like this…what is it, this Ibrahim?

I'll tell you. Because you're so curious.

A person who knows they will die at another's hands does not usually run and scream, like you'd think. What they do is they get incredibly sleepy. That is all, like moving is too much an effort. They lay down, their faces get very very sleepy and sad. That is all. *(Silence.)* So this Mlatko fellow. The story sounds…possible. But very…dramatic. And I never met him. *(He sits back at the table.)* What, you don't believe me?

(Long pause. Everyone stares at him.)

ELENA: *(Softly.)* Kako si izgubio ruku, Juraj? [How did you lose your hand, Juraj?]

JURAJ: I told you, it was a grenade! You all want to know how I lost my hand? *(Silence, then Juraj smiles, starts to laugh. A joke.)* They took it at customs, what do you think?

(Beat.)

ELENA: Look my brother's name is Juraj, it always has been. *(Beat, to Dick.)* Dick you know that.

DICK: *(Pause, then.)* Of course.

ELENA: And he's never been married, I would know.

JOHN: It's just, uhhh, Ev just has this great memory for tragic news articles.

EVAN: *(Soft.)* It's a gift.

DICK: You are just Holocaust obsessed, Evan, if you don't mind me saying.

EVAN: What?

DICK: Oh come on I remember when you saw "Schindler's List."

JOHN: *(Laughs.)* That's true.

EVAN: *(A reprimand.)* John— *(Beat, then.)* Juraj I was just curious that's all. I didn't offend you did I? The story…it just…stayed with me, that's all.

DICK: *(To Evan.)* Didn't you write words to the theme from "Schindler's List" too? I'm not making this up.

ELENA: Dick Dick stop…

JOHN: Well you did, Evan.

DICK: And, uh, we were laughing for like two weeks in the faculty lounge with your idea for the Schindler's List lunch boxes and action figures, right? And, and the dream house commercial: *(In little kids voice.)* Mommy I want a Plaszow Labor Camp set with real crematoria! *(In hushed, very rapid, very low, "end of a Mattel commercial" voice.)* Jews not included. Come on Evan these are your jokes.

ELENA: Dick stop.

EVAN: *I* made these jokes. Me. You have no right—

DICK: *(Overlapping.)* What what because *your* grandfather it's okay to—

ELENA: *(Overlapping.)* Dick—

EVAN: *(Overlapping.)* Okay Dick just leave me alone—

JURAJ: Evan. You want to touch it? It's not that scary. *(Juraj holds his arm out.)*

ELENA: Juraj, Nemoj. [Juraj, no.]

JURAJ: Come on, I am asking you.

> *(Evan pauses, then slowly reaches, then suddenly grasps, feels. A strangely intimate moment. They stare at each other.)*

EVAN: Yeah. It's an arm. Not scary at all. *(Brightens up.)* God I am starving all of a sudden.

DICK: Seconds for me, Lena.

JOHN: You know I feel bad. We should all go see a show or something this week.

EVAN: *(To Juraj.)* You should come in Monday and see John about giving you a recommendation.

JOHN: Yeah sure…I can't make promises but I can see what I can do.

ELENA: Did you hear that Juraj? You're to see John tomorrow in his office. Juraj?

JURAJ: My gift. I should open my gift. *(He crosses to a side table where the gift box is. He opens it, takes out a bottle of wine, looks at it.)*

JOHN: It's wine.

JURAJ: Moravian wine, my favorite.

ELENA: *(Beat.)* What's wrong?

JURAJ: Nothing. This was very nice. It's just—this is so nice. *(Beat.)* For a moment this felt like home. *(He looks at Evan, then his sister.)* *(Lights fade to black.)*

END OF PLAY